D0083465

CHRISTOPHER MARLOWE

WORLD DRAMATISTS

CHRISTOPHER

ARLOWE

GERALD PINCISS

WITH HALFTONE ILLUSTRATIONS

26536

FREDERICK UNGAR PUBLISHING CO.
NEW YORK

Copyright © 1975 by Frederick Ungar Publishing Co., Inc.
Printed in the United States of America
Library of Congress Catalog Card Number: 72-79934
Designed by Edith Fowler
ISBN: 0-8044-2694-5

CONTENTS

CHRONOLOGY

1564:   *26 February*. Christopher Marlowe is chris-
           tened in the church of St. George the
           Martyr, Canterbury, the son of John Mar-
           lowe, shoemaker and bondsman, and Kath-
           arine Arthur.

1579:   *14 January*. Enters the King's School, Can-
           terbury, as a King's scholar.

1580:   *December*. Is in residence at Corpus Christi
           College, Cambridge University, as a Canter-
           bury scholar holding a fellowship founded
           by Archbishop Parker. The scholarship is
           tenable for six years if the candidate intends
           to enter holy orders.

1584:   Is awarded B.A. degree.

1584–85:   Attends Corpus Christi College erratically,
           with long periods of absence.

1587:   *March*. Marlowe's petition for his M.A. is
           denied by Cambridge.

           29 June. The Privy Council issues a direc-
           tive to the university ordering that Mar-
           lowe's degree be conferred.

> Whereas it was reported that Christopher
> Morley was determined to haue gone be-
> yond the seas to Reames [Rheims] and there
> to remain, their Lordships thought good to
> certify that he had no such intent, but that
> in all his accions he had behaued him selfe
> orderlie and discreetelie wherebe he had

done her Majesty good service, and deserued to be rewarded for his faithfull dealinge. Their Lordships' request was that the rumor thereof should be allaied by all possible meanes, and that he should be furthered in the degree he was to take this next Commencement: Because it was not her Majesty's pleasure that any one employed as he had been in matters touching the benefitt of his countrie should be defamed by those who are ignorant in th'affaires he went about.[1]

Marlowe is established in London.

1588: The playwright Robert Greene attacks *Tamburlaine* in his *Perimedes*: "I could not make my verses jet upon the stage in tragical buskins, every word filling the mouth like a fa-burden of Bow-bells, daring God out of heaven with that atheist Tamburlaine." Greene alludes to Marlowe himself when describing "such mad and scoffing poets that have poetical spirits as bred of Merlin's race, if there be any in England." The pun refers to the form of Marlowe's name, "Marlin," most frequently used at Cambridge.

1589: Greene renews the attack on Marlowe, in *Menaphon*, by his sarcastic reference to a "Canterbury tale" told by a "propheticall full mouth that as he were a Cobbler's eldest sonne, would by the laste tell where another's shoe wrings."

1589: *18 September.* William Bradley, who earlier petitioned the Queen's Bench for security against attack by Marlowe's friend, the poet Thomas Watson, and others, meets Marlowe in Hog Lane. The two begin fighting, and when Watson arrives, Bradley takes up the quarrel with him. In the course of the duel, Bradley is killed and Marlowe and Watson are arrested and locked in Newgate Prison.

Marlowe is released on 1 October, after spending thirteen days in jail.

3 December. Watson and Marlowe appear before the justices at the Old Bailey. Marlowe is dismissed, and Watson claims murder in self-defense and is pardoned.

1592:   Two constables petition that Marlowe be sworn to keep the peace.

1593:   *18 May.* The Privy Council, investigating charges of heresy and treason, issues a warrant to Henry Maunder, "one of the Messengers of Her Majesty's Chamber, to repaire to the house of Mr. Thomas Walsingham in Kent, or to anie other place where he shall understand Christofer Marlow to be remayning, and by vertue thereof to apprehend and bring him to the Court in his companie."

20 May. Marlowe announces his readiness to answer the charges.

30 May. Marlowe is killed at Deptford. According to the inquisition held two days after Marlowe's death, Marlowe had met Ingram Frizer, Nicholas Skeres, and Robert Poley

> . . . & after supper the said Ingram & Christopher Morley were in speech & uttered one to the other divers malicious words for the reason that they could not be at one nor agree about the payment of the sum of pence, that is *le recknynge*, there: & the said Christopher Morley then lying upon a bed in the room where they supped, & moved with anger against the said Ingram ffrysar . . . and the said Ingram then & there sitting in the room aforesaid with his back towards the bed where the said Christopher Morley was then lying . . . & with the front part of his body towards the table & the aforesaid Nicholas Skeres & Robert Poley sitting on either side of the said Ingram in such a manner that the same Ingram ffrysar in no wise could take flight: it so befell that the said Christopher

Morley on a sudden & of his malice towards the said Ingram aforethought, then & there maliciously drew the dagger of the said Ingram which was at his back, and with the same dagger the said Christopher Morley then & there maliciously gave the aforesaid Ingram two wounds on his head of the length of two inches & of the depth of a quarter of an inch; whereupon the said Ingram, in fear of being slain . . . in his own defense & for the saving of his life, then & there struggled with the said Christopher Morley to get back from him his dagger aforesaid: in which affray the same Ingram could not get away from the said Christopher Morley; and so it befell in that affray that the said Ingram, in defense of his life, with the dagger aforesaid of the value of 12d. gave the said Christopher Morley then & there a mortal wound over his right eye of the depth of two inches & of the width of one inch; of which mortal wound the aforesaid Christopher Morley then & there instantly died.[2]

MARLOWE AND
ELIZABETHAN THEATER

1. The Elizabethan Stage

By the mid-1580s when Marlowe took up residence in London, the professional theater was already a well-established enterprise. James Burbage had built the first playhouse in 1576, designing a structure that was inspired partly by the open-roofed, galleried inn yard, and partly by the bear-baiting arena. Another playhouse, the Curtain, was soon erected nearby, and stage performances became an even more commercial and professional activity. These theaters were located in Shoreditch, a suburb north of the city, close enough to the center of population not to be too inconvenient, yet beyond the direct control of those middle-class shopkeepers and Puritans such as the Lord Mayor and Aldermen who disapproved of the theater and the temptations and distractions it offered.

Despite this disapproval, theater was a highly popular diversion, and playgoing was not strongly resisted. About thirteen percent of the population went to the playhouses each week, making an average daily attendance at the theaters total close to twenty-five hundred spectators.[1] And this audience was a representative cross section of English society; the actors had to appeal to a diverse clientele. Once, when the playhouses were searched for military impressment, they were found filled not simply with the idle, loose-living, or dissolute, but with gentlemen, servingmen, lawyers, clerks, country men with law cases, "aye the Quenes men, knightes and as it was credibly reported one Earle."

In fact, Queen Elizabeth herself delighted in watching stage performances and even licensed a troupe as her royal players; in 1583 the Privy Council enfranchised twelve actors, an unusually large number for a company, to travel and perform in order that they maintain "dexteritie and perfection," enabling them to appear before Her Majesty for her recreation and delight. The royal franchise gave not only the company but also the profession itself more dignity and security. Troupes had even before this been invited to appear before their monarch as part of the festivities during the Christmas season, and their talents were employed also when court entertainments were required.

Performances at court were elaborate, especially when the resources of the royal agent, the Master of the Revels, were available. But public performances were also both eye and ear filling. On tour during the summer months, traveling players appeared in the provinces on improvised stages with the more limited variety of costumes and properties they carried with them. In London, however, performing in theaters equipped with special facilities—pulleys, traps, sound-effect chambers, and changing rooms—the players made a striking impression. Elaborate costuming was a frequent expense, for Elizabethans were fond of clothes, and audiences appreciated the richness of the players' apparel. Stage properties were numerous: one inventory includes such items as dragons, lions, Cerberus with his three heads, a tree of golden apples, and a great horse. The stage itself was draped with painted cloths such as one that depicted the sun and moon, a motif repeated on the underside of the canopy covering a portion of the stage.

The most thorough information on equipment, repertory, and box-office receipts is to be found today in a diary that was kept intermittently by Philip Henslowe, a theatrical entrepreneur. Henslowe was the owner of the Rose Theater and the father-in-law of one of the most famous actors of the day, Edward Alleyn. In fact, Alleyn's company, the Admiral's Men, was one of the two principal adult troupes. In most adult companies a number of actor-sharers jointly owned the company's stock of plays, costumes, and properties. They employed some hired men and boys to fill out their numbers and play women's roles; and they worked in a theater owned by a business manager, like James Burbage or Henslowe, who took half the receipts in the galleries at each performance.

The two major adult companies, the Admiral's Men and the Chamberlain's Men, performed in London every day except Sunday and during Lent. At Christmas they vied for court invitations, and during the summer, when the warm weather threatened an outbreak of the plague, they toured in the country. The size of the repertory and the demand for new material is astonishing. In a three-year period in the last decade of the sixteenth century, a leading actor had to remember some seventy different roles, learning some fifty-two or fifty-three during those three years alone.[2]

Plays were usually bought outright from their

authors, generally for the rather insubstantial sum of five pounds. Any play performed a dozen times achieved very respectable success; and no play in Henslowe's records received more than thirty-two performances. It is understandable that most of the plays of this period have been lost: either lack of interest in such ephemeral texts or the desire of a company to retain control over the script meant that many works were never printed, and even many of those printed have not survived. With the exception of Ben Jonson, few authors were concerned with the publication of their dramatic writing. Shakespeare, who never oversaw the printing of a single play, was typical.

The varied skills of the actors matched the diversity of their repertory. They were prepared to appear in works based on English or French history, or on legend and folk tales; in comedies, romantic, satiric, pastoral; in tragedies classical and factual; in Biblical stories and quasi-allegorical spectacles; and they were prepared to perform fencing exhibitions, tumbling, jigs, and poetic improvisations. Their acting style might seem to us flamboyant, bombastic, and oratorical, yet so severe a critic as Ben Jonson thought that in Alleyn's abilities "present worth in all dost so contract,/ As others speake, but onely thou dost act."[3] Another commented that Alleyn "so acting to the life . . . made any part (especially a majestic one) to become him." Marlowe was clearly fortunate to have had Alleyn portray Tamburlaine, Faustus, and Barabas.

The children's companies, choir boys at St. Paul's or at the Chapel Royal, offered a more expensive, refined, and aristocratic alternative to the robust, popular entertainments of the adult companies. In smaller, roofed, private theaters before a more wealthy and sophisticated audience, the children appeared two or three days a week in works generally distinguished by a concern with elegant staging and music as well as delicacy of sentiment and expression. The acting record of the children's companies is unfortunately less complete than that of the adult troupes.

2. Marlowe's Life and Career

Although there is no question of the importance of Marlowe's contribution to English theater, there is uncertainty about the facts of his life. Despite the wealth of details—much more is known about Marlowe's life than has been learned about many of his contemporaries who wrote for the stage—questions of interpretation and of reliability persist.

It is impossible, for example, to know how much weight to give some of the comments about Marlowe by his contemporaries. The playwright Thomas Kyd, with whom he shared a room for a time, claimed that Marlowe, "intemperate & of a cruel hart," was rash "in attempting soden pryvie injuries to men." But Kyd was himself under government investigation when he said this, and he could easily have intended to shift suspicion to Marlowe, who was already dead.

The Baines document, a note to the Privy Council accusing Marlowe of heresy and treason, is also of questionable reliability. Baines himself may have been the criminal by that name who was later hanged at Tyburn. And, what is of more importance, if Marlowe had uttered heretical or treasonous remarks they may well not have been said in sincerity. It is, after all, entirely possible that a bright, high-spirited, young man with theological training entertained himself and his friends with arguments that exercised their wit and titillated their sensibilities, but that were not held with any conviction. Marlowe's words may have been entirely misunderstood by the less imaginative and less intellectual Baines; shocking Baines may, indeed, have been the very aim of Marlowe's conversation and the source of his pleasure.

Finally, Ingram Frizer's account of the stabbing of Marlowe is problematic on several counts. The witnesses and participants were hardly the most trustworthy individuals: Skeres was listed in 1585 among "Masterless men and cutpurses," and was arrested several times for sedition; Poley, originally a Catholic, had been a double agent in the Babington plot, which led to the execution of Mary, Queen of Scots; and Frizer, who had a record for sharp practices and contentious behavior, was a servant of Thomas Walsingham, the secretary of the Privy Council and head of the government's intelligence network. The scene the three men described at the inquisition is difficult to accept fully. Why did neither Poley nor Skeres intervene in the quarrel between Marlowe and Frizer? Why did Frizer present his back and his weapon to the man with whom he was quarreling? Why was instant death claimed for Marlowe when, according to medical authorities, a wound "over the right eye of the depth of two inches & of the width of one inch" could cause only a coma? Their account raises more questions than it answers.

Despite our inability to resolve these facts, a sense of the playwright still begins to emerge. Surely something essential about him can be detected from his friendship with literary and intellectual men such as Thomas Watson and Thomas Kyd, Sir Walter Raleigh and Thomas Harriot; from his intimacy with aristocrats such as Francis Walsingham; and from his associations with high and low government agents. Quick-tempered, bold, daring, aggressive, intelligent— these were characteristics of his personality. And his plays are extensions and expressions of his mind. Their substance comes out of those intellectual currents Marlowe found intriguing and fashionable, shaped in a manner that would excite an audience, and, at the same time, pass the censor. Skepticism, nationalism, heroism, the opposition of the Christian humanism of the Anglican Church and the new philosophy of science and materialism, the joy of molding a verse form and the delight in shaping a dramatic structure that could thrill a motley crowd—all aroused his interest.

The chronology of Marlowe's plays is impossible to determine with any certainty; factual evidence, topical allusions, and even judgments of style all provide inconclusive data. Marlowe's poems, too, are nearly as difficult to date as his plays. His translation of the first book of Lucan's *Pharsalia*, on the wars between Caesar and Pompey, is possibly an early attempt to handle nondramatic blank verse, but his version of Ovid's *Amores* might have been undertaken either during his Cambridge days or much later. And the date of composition of *Hero and Leander*, his splendid but unfinished Ovidian erotic poem, is also unclear.

Among the plays *Tamburlaine the Great*, Part I, Marlowe's first great success, is generally believed by most Marlowe scholars to have followed the writing of *Dido, Queen of Carthage*, which was probably composed about 1586. *Tamburlaine* was widely known by 1588, and most likely had been drafted by the time Marlowe was leaving Cambridge. If *Tamburlaine the Great*, Part II, is indeed a sequel, as is claimed on the title page, then it was probably in progress in 1588 in response to the success of Part I. *The Jew of Malta* is the most likely of Marlowe's plays to have followed the two *Tamburlaine* plays: the text was in the acting repertory by 1591, and the prologue reference to the death of the Duke of Guise dates at least that part of the play after 1588, when the Guise was murdered at Blois.

There is reasonable certainty about the date of composition of *The Massacre at Paris*. Henslowe noted in his *Diary* that the work was "ne" on 26 January 1593. If this abbreviation is an indication of a first performance, as is generally believed, Marlowe's historical play would have been completed not long before the Henslowe entry.

Dating the writing of *Doctor Faustus* with any degree of assurance is impossible. Settling on the year 1592 for the composition of the play at least allows time for Marlowe's source, the *Faustbuch*, to have appeared in English translation. And accepting this date also places the drama, notable for its intellectual and literary sophistication, later rather than earlier in Marlowe's career. Since the play exists in two widely differing versions, however, it is dangerous to give too much weight to stylistic or textual arguments that attempt to determine the date of the writing by judgments about the maturity of style or technique.

If not Marlowe's last completed play, *Edward II* was surely finished very late in his career. Since the title page of the 1594 quarto claims it was acted by Pembroke's Men, who reopened in London during the winter of 1592–93, the play was probably written very shortly before their appearance.

Marlowe's works are all the products of a sensitive and imaginative mind and an extraordinary poetic talent. He brought to English poetry a feeling of ease and excitement that had been unexpressed before. His development of and contribution to the blank-verse line can be recognized simply by considering his use of it in a variety of works and comparing these with the writings of his predecessors.

Closely examining a passage of blank verse in a pre-Marlovian play will highlight the qualities of Marlowe's writing even more distinctly. A speech in the first blank-verse tragedy, *Gorboduc* (1561), by Thomas Sackville and Thomas Norton, will serve for contrast. Porrex, having just murdered his brother, confronts his father:

> If ever grief, if ever woeful man
> Might move regret with sorrow of his fault,
> I think the torment of my mournful case,
> Known to your grace, as I do feel the same,
> Would force even Wrath herself to pity me.
> But as the water, troubled with the mud,
> Shows not the face which else the eye should see,
> Even so your ireful mind with stirred thought
> Cannot so perfectly discern my cause.
> But this unhap, amongst so many heaps,
> I must content me with, most wretched man,
> That to myself I must reserve my woe.

Though Porrex may claim he is grief-stricken, he is not very convincing. The regularity of the iambs belies any deep emotion; and the caesura interrupts the flow of his words, contradicting his claim to intense distress. His image also is too studied for one in such anguish. Nothing approaching passion has interfered with the steady production of these pentameter lines; the feeling has only been described, not reinforced by the rhythm of his words.

Tamburlaine, describing his grief over the death of Zenocrate, also speaks in lines of nearly perfect iambic pentameter, but in his words there is freedom of accent, variety of sentence structure, and attention to sound.

> What, is she dead? Techelles, draw thy sword
> And wound the earth, that it may cleave in twain
> And we descend into th'infernal vaults,
> To hale the Fatal Sisters by the hair
> And throw them in the triple moat of hell,
> For taking hence my fair Zenocrate.
> Casane and Theridamas, to arms!
> Raise cavalieros higher than the clouds,
> And with the cannon break the frame of heaven.*

Tamburlaine's grief is mixed with anger and combativeness. Scansion reveals that both at the very beginning and end of the speech the standard iambic pattern is broken. Tamburlaine's words open with a trochee, the variation conveying the sense of the speaker's deep emotion, and his last line, with its feminine ending, gives a sense of lightness to the rhythm. The four sentences of his lament are respectively interrogative, declarative, hortatory, and imperative; two are simple, another complex, and the last, compound. Incorporating the nouns of address into the lines gives direction and immediacy to the speaker's words, and their multisyllabic sounds add richness as well as drama. Assonance and alliteration are modulated so that sound supports the emotional overtones: "dead," "earth," "cleave"; or "hale," "hell," "hence." The triple alliteration of "cavalieros," "clouds," and "cannon" gives the conclusion of the address force and boldness, a sense of deep conviction that would be hampered by strict adherence to any formula.

---

* All quotations from the plays are taken from Irving Ribner's edition, *The Complete Plays of Christopher Marlowe* (New York, 1963).

A few lines from *Edward II* provide another example of Marlowe's control over his verse and his increasingly subtle adjustment of the rhythmic pattern to express character and emotion as well as story. Edward's words to the Abbot of Neath, who offers him shelter from his pursuing enemies, are full of sorrow, grief, self-indulgence, and self-dramatization.

> Whilom I was powerful and full of pomp;
> But what is he whom rule and empery
> Have not in life or death made miserable?
> Come, Spencer; come Baldock, come, sit down by
>   me;
> Make trial now of that philosophy
> That in our famous nurseries of arts
> Thou sucked'st from Plato and from Aristotle.
> Father, this life contemplative is heaven.
> O that I might this life in quiet lead.

Although this is not Marlowe's most intense or powerful poetry, even this short speech, filled as it is with traditional clichés, is superior to what Marlowe's contemporaries generally were writing. The first line opens with an extra accent; line four, Edward's call to his two friends to join him, is an irregular line of dactyllic tetrameter; the next to last line opens with a trochee, and this one and the line before it both have feminine endings. In this passage the iambic pentameter line is a kind of standard against which these variations are played to suggest the movement of the speaker's mind and the emotional pitch of his feelings. And these are reenforced by the simplicity of his diction.

Marlowe succeeded in demonstrating more powerfully than any earlier writer in English drama the adaptability and strength of blank verse. Variations from the basic iambic foot establish a counterrhythm that approaches natural inflection and persuades the listener of the sincerity of the emotion in the words. Flexibility not only in feet but also in meter—alexandrines, tetrameters, nine-syllable lines—sensitivity to the sound value of the language, and, finally, careful control over enjambment and caesura are the major elements of Marlowe's writing at its best.

Although Marlowe's intellect and talent matured rapidly, there was a general consistency in his attitude. Irony was Marlowe's most popular mode; skepticism, detachment, a sensibility that finds another's pain the subject for laughter, were characteristics of his disposition. He was not interested in innocent delights; the pleasures of sincere affection are typical of those subjects that were uncongenial for him, yet not remote from his subject matter.

Marlowe's dramas are powerful and effective. The technique in all of them is basically the same: to set two irreconcilable positions in conflict, and structure the play out of the struggle between them. The plays, however, were intended to raise questions of morality and ethics, not to answer them. In fact, the drama may very often work to prevent the audience from wholehearted identification with any point of view: Edward may be a frivolous king, but he is also a sympathetic victim; Barabas may be a villain, but so, it seems, is just about everyone else on Malta; Tamburlaine may be glorious or just vaingloriously cruel. Man's frailty, the nature and the meaning of existence, the individual's experience of guilt, anxiety, and suffering—these are the threads out of which tragedies are woven, and they can all be found in the fabric of the greatest pre-Shakespearean English dramatist.

THE PLAYS

Tamburlaine the Great, PART I

Although in many ways it is the least complex of Marlowe's plays, *Tamburlaine the Great* may
well be the most striking. With it, Marlowe made of
his predecessors and his contemporaries in the Elizabethan theater foils for heightening the excitement
and brilliance of his own work. After the preciosity
of Lyly, the bombast of Greene, and the rhetoric of
Kyd, Marlowe's skills as a playwright stood out even
more sharply. The range and versatility he displayed
in the manipulation of his medium is astonishing.
Furthermore, it is clear that Marlowe himself recognized his genius, proclaiming it with arrogance and
boldness. With an ear for lyric poetry and impas-
sioned speech, and an eye for stage effects, he naturally
became a successful dramatist.

The success of *Tamburlaine the Great*, however,
can be explained only partly by language and spectacle.
Marlowe generated additional audience interest by
incorporating in his work issues of philosophical, religious, and political importance. He realized that a
conflict of views on power, morality, providence, or
true nobility, left unresolved, can provide an exciting

intellectual resonance to the struggle unfolding in the story. This is the case with *Tamburlaine*. Its appeal is threefold, and to the most curious spectators the visual and aural elements may be the least interesting.

The play opens with a prologue, a favorite Marlowe device, and the eight lines of this introduction establish the subject, treatment, and mood of the work. Even in so brief a passage one can recognize the characteristics distinctive of Marlowe's style: the heavy use of gerunds and the careful balancing of phrases.

> Threat'ning the world with high astounding terms
> And scourging kingdoms with his conquering sword.

What is more, the personality of the playwright—an independence approaching belligerence—is made clear from the start. In his work one will not find those effects of hack writers who pass off horseplay as wit or unscannable verse as poetry. From Marlowe there came no plea for indulgence, no request to piece out his imperfections with imagination. The audience is asked only to look at Tamburlaine: "View but his picture in this tragic glass/ And then applaud his fortunes as you please."

Marlowe's self-appreciation, although it may not make him sympathetic, is understandable, for his were abilities much prized by the educated Elizabethan. His skill in using language and his control over the devices of argument were highly valued in England. They formed no small part of the Renaissance academic curriculum. Since it was thought that the study of such classical orators as Cicero would help form the moral man, and that the moral man would be able to move others to imitate the good, the principles of rhetoric, the organization of speeches, and the techniques of embellishing phrases were adapted from classical precedents into English as part of the general educational process. Although such attitudes might open the way for demagogues and sophists, the Renaissance Englishman nevertheless believed the hero, the man of magnanimity, could be identified not simply by what he said, but by his manner and the persuasiveness with which he spoke. The great man was expected to be powerful at convincing others. The skills of the politician and the poet were closely allied. Perhaps these beliefs and their durability will be less surprising if we remember that Cromwell chose Milton as his Latin secretary when Latin was still the official diplomatic language.

From the very beginning of *Tamburlaine the Great*, the ability to use language serves as an important index to character. Mycetes, the King of Persia, announces in the opening lines of the first scene that he is "agrieved,/ Yet insufficient to express the same." Mycetes is weak and stupid and his inability to produce a "great and thundr'ing speech" betrays his cowardice, just as his mixed metaphors reveal how illogically he thinks. Indeed, before the scene is over, Mycetes's brother, Cosroe, has decided to overthrow him and join with the Persian army marching against the Scythian shepherd, Tamburlaine, and his forces.

Marlowe thus presents two characters who will stand in contrast to the heroism and nobility of Tamburlaine: one, a king by birth, is incapable of ruling—heredity is surely not always the best determinant of rulers—and the other, Cosroe, rebels, proclaiming himself emperor. When Tamburlaine later attains the throne, he will not deserve a brother's curses.

Tamburlaine is introduced in the second scene. He has just captured Zenocrate, the daughter of the Soldan of Egypt, and, announcing his love for her, he strips off his shepherd's clothes and stands dressed in complete armor. With unshakable self-confidence he declares that Zenocrate will marry him and that he will rule the world. This combination is apt, for Tamburlaine's love for Zenocrate will spur his ambition. Were Marlowe's powerful verse less convincing, Tamburlaine's promises would sound hollow; but no listener's skepticism can hold out against the self-assurance of his language, or the attractiveness of his lyricism. And if his words alone fail to convince Zenocrate of his valor, she can watch his performance as he confronts Theridamas, the captain of a thousand Persian horsemen.

Once he has seen Tamburlaine, Theridamas remarks that the shepherd's face may truly be the mirror of his mind. This notion of the validity of physiognomy, the science of reading the correspondence between character and appearance, was popularly accepted in Elizabethan England. Of Tamburlaine, Theridamas observes: "His looks do menace heaven and dare the gods." Tamburlaine, studying the Persian's expression, returns the compliment:

> Art thou but captain of a thousand horse,
> That by characters graven in thy brows,
> And by thy martial face and stout aspect,
> Deserv'st to have the leading of an host?
> Forsake thy king and do but join with me,
> And we will triumph over all the world.

Tamburlaine's arguments are overwhelming: "won with thy words and conquered with thy looks," Theridamas yields to him. With Theridamas converting to the ranks of Tamburlaine's admirers, Zenocrate's begrudging acceptance of her situation, which closes the act, strikes one as an expression more of maidenly modesty than of genuine disapproval.

Act II builds immediately toward a double climax: the defeat of the foolish Mycetes by the united forces of Tamburlaine and Cosroe, then the defeat of Cosroe by Tamburlaine and his followers. Marlowe heightens the stature of his hero by describing his appearance and strength, by recounting his powers, and by emphasizing the nobility of his attitude. Tamburlaine does not steal the crown from Mycetes, but "pull[s] it" from his head; he does not play lord regent to Cosroe, but proclaims himself emperor; he does not attack Cosroe's army without warning, but "bid[s] him turn him back to war with us,/ That only made him king to make us sport."

With his last breath Cosroe calls Tamburlaine and his captains "the strangest men that ever nature made!" Others have boasted that they controlled their fates; others have bragged of their inviolable will, but such claims were always ultimately negated. Eventually fortune's wheel turned and she found a new favorite; or, from another viewpoint, providential guidance, using fortune as its instrument, intervened and altered the course of events. When Tamburlaine claimed to "hold the Fates bound fast in iron chains," his words first sounded like braggadocio, but to the dying Cosroe they now seem to describe an amazing truth. Tamburlaine's claim is not unique, but the truth in the claim is.

Cosroe is right; Tamburlaine and his fellows are the strangest men. And they are marked as special not simply by their unprecedented successes but also by their embodiment of a new conception of life. Renaissance science argued that physical and psychological well-being was achieved by a perfect balance of the elements in man's constitution, but Tamburlaine argues that only when the elements are in an imbalance, each constantly struggling for supremacy, is man healthy. He presents a new philosophy of human nature: that man is by definition a quarrelsome and fighting animal, that energy, vitality, insatiability describe the essence of his life, that it is unnatural for him to be contented. The gods themselves set the precedent, he points out, for Jove thrust his father from the seat of power.

> Nature, that framed us of four elements
> Warring within our breasts for regiment,
> Doth teach us all to have aspiring minds.
> Our souls, whose faculties can comprehend
> The wondrous architecture of the world
> And measure every wandering planet's course,
> Still climbing after knowledge infinite,
> And always moving as the restless spheres,
> Wills us to wear ourselves and never rest,
> Until we reach the ripest fruit of all,
> That perfect bliss and sole felicity,
> The sweet fruition of an earthly crown.

Even Tamburlaine's conclusion is shocking. The greatest prize, the most lofty goal for Tamburlaine, is temporal, physical, and worldly, not spiritual or religious. A heavenly crown, not an "earthly" one is a more appropriate symbol of "perfect bliss" and "sole felicity"; Tamburlaine's ethics are as iconoclastic as his philosophy.

The defeat of Mycetes and Cosroe is just the first rung on the ladder of Tamburlaine's conquests; the Persian empire, acquired by the end of Act II, will prove to have been the least difficult of Tamburlaine's victories, its former kings the easiest to subdue. The more challenging defeat of Bajazeth, Emperor of the Turks and ruler of Africa, is the subject of Act III.

Bajazeth's plans for attacking Constantinople show him to be a more formidable opponent; his strategy is more refined than any of the military tactics the Persians were capable of formulating. When the truce that Bajazeth offers Tamburlaine is promptly rejected, battle follows.

The thousand men of Mycetes, the twenty thousand of Cosroe, are nothing compared to the size of Bajazeth's army: he can draw on twice ten thousand mounted janissaries and two hundred thousand footmen. Yet all of these will be lost in the struggle with Tamburlaine's forces; Tamburlaine will be victorious.

Even Zenocrate, now acknowledging her attraction to her captor, defends Tamburlaine against the criticism of her servant and the vaunting of Zabina, the wife of Bajazeth. While the battle rages offstage the two women scold each other like fishwives. Tamburlaine then encounters Bajazeth, subdues him before the women, and orders Zenocrate crowned with Zabina's diadem.

Marlowe succeeded in raising the tension of the play by providing blank verse that is alternately militaristic and lyric, by dramatizing Tamburlaine's continued defiance of any superior power, and by increasing the stakes of every battle. Act III closes as Tamburlaine defies those armies of Africa and Greece that threaten to come to aid Bajazeth. He announces that his fleet will cover the waters of the world; from the Mediterranean to the Indian Ocean, across the Pacific and the Atlantic back to the Straits of Gibraltar, his ships "shall meet and join their force in one. . . . And by this means I'll win the world at last."

The movement of the play through the end of Act IV is uncomplicated: a succession of increasingly more stunning victories follows for Tamburlaine. Any lack of suspense is compensated for by the steady growth in the scope of the action. Despite the episodic nature of the plot, moving from one completed incident to another, the unity of the work is sustained by its concentration on a central figure.

With Act IV Marlowe prepares the audience for the final resolution of the drama. Tamburlaine, laying siege to Damascus, will oppose the Soldan, Zenocrate's father. The ludicrous tormenting of Bajazeth and the spectacular crowning of Tamburlaine's three generals offer variety to the ensuing action, but the subject of main concern is still the hero's war policy. Despite the threats of the Soldan and of the imprisoned Bajazeth, Tamburlaine remains undaunted. The warning that "Ambitious pride shall make thee fall," the old cry of hubris, with its expectations of imminent disaster, is raised here only to be unfulfilled. Tamburlaine seems justified in claiming that "The chiefest god . . . Will sooner burn the glorious frame of heaven/ Than it should so conspire my overthrow." He enjoys the curses of his enemies, for his pleasure comes from "Having the power from the imperial heaven/ To turn them all upon their proper heads."

Invincible and inexorable, Tamburlaine cannot compromise his desire to rule the world. Even Zenocrate cannot persuade him to make peace with her father: "And wouldst thou have me buy thy father's love/ With such a loss?" he asks. Surely it is his very strength and power that attracts her, and, presumably, will earn the respect of the Soldan himself. Tamburlaine's promise of safety to the father and friends of his future wife, "If with their lives they will be pleased to yield," is all that his honor will allow. For him, honor and value are determined not by birth but by accomplishment, stamina, and success. Tamburlaine measures true nobility by deeds. He takes pride in his shepherd origins and tells his followers, "Your births shall be no blemish to your fame,/ For virtue is the fount whence honor springs."

The last act opens as Tamburlaine, unable to yield to Zenocrate's pleas, lays siege to Damascus. He and his armies are now clothed in black, indicating that all the city's inhabitants must die: "that which mine honor swears shall be performed." He must keep his word even when he prefers not to. Remorselessness and power are inseparable qualities for a man of his character and ambition. Flexibility is impossible.

When Tamburlaine appears, however, he is melancholy, perhaps due in part to the resistance of Damascus and to the killings this will force him to commit. But in large measure his mood is in response to the anguish of Zenocrate, torn between love for him and love for her country and father. For the first time in the play, Marlowe attempts, in however rudimentary a fashion, to locate the struggle within the hero himself; the opposition here is not between Tamburlaine and some easily overpowered external force, but inside his divided mind. His indecision is both new and troubling to him; the struggle of his "tempted thoughts" to yield to the will of his beloved, unlike the more physical kind of combat, is a "doubtful battle." Zenocrate's torment over his impending attack on the Soldan causes Tamburlaine more agony than will his army the people of Damascus—or so he claims.

His concern for Zenocrate's feeling is the occasion for one of Tamburlaine's most magniloquent passages, fourteen lines describing the ineffable quality of beauty. Tamburlaine's soliloquy attempts to analyze why Zenocrate, the embodiment of all that is beautiful, holds such power over him.

What is beauty, saith my sufferings, then?
If all the pens that ever poets held
Had fed the feelings of their master's thoughts,
And every sweetness that inspired their hearts,
Their minds, and muses on admirèd themes;
If all the heavenly quintessence they still
From their immortal flowers of poesy,
Wherein, as in a mirror, we perceive
The highest reaches of a human wit;
If these had made one poem's period,
And all combined in beauty's worthiness
Yet should there hover in their restless heads
One thought, one grace, one wonder, at the least,
Which into words no virtue can digest.

Tamburlaine attempts to define the quality of his emotional response to beauty by offering three hypothetical comparisons. Even in their cumulative effect, however, even in what could be the most perfect product of the most talented writer, "one thought, one grace, one wonder, at the least" would still escape inclusion.

Tamburlaine discovers the resolution of his dilemma, reconciling the claims of his military goals and of his beautiful Zenocrate, when he recognizes that as hero, as generator of fame, valor, and victory, beauty must celebrate him for his accomplishments: the reason for arousing beauty, the magnet for attracting it, and the power for subduing it reside in him. And by fulfilling this role, he expects to find true glory.

After Tamburlaine exits to battle the forces of the Soldan, the stage is left to Bajazeth and Zabina. Now that the martial music is over and the lyric mood has passed, Marlowe offers his audience the poetry of curses. Imprisoned like a savage animal and used as a footstool by Tamburlaine, Bajazeth damns his captor in a frenzy of Senecan inspiration. Acknowledging that he is powerless to regain his freedom, in despair he dashes out his brains against the iron ribs of his cage. Zabina goes mad—"Hell, death, Tamburlaine, hell! Make ready my coach, my chair, my jewels. I come, I come, I come!"—and follows her husband's precedent. All this is spectacular diversion. Bajazeth and Zabina are, after all, seldom sympathetic characters on stage. Their function is threefold: to magnify Tamburlaine's stature, to grant Marlowe an opportunity to exercise his own peculiarly cruel sense of humor, and to delight the Elizabethans, who relished just such episodes of death and madness.

This scene is followed by Zenocrate's formal lament. Her set piece—with its criticism of the indifference of earth and heaven, with its refrain of "Behold the Turk and his great Empress," and with its observations on the insecurity of worldly success—ends on a plea for forgiveness for Tamburlaine and herself. From whom Zenocrate begs pardon is not clear, since Tamburlaine's actions seem to have won divine approval; indeed, her maid immediately reminds her that Tamburlaine has fortune at his command.

Zenocrate's remorse and fear of disaster are unfounded. Tamburlaine is once again victorious, but this time he returns to her conquered father, the Soldan, all that he has just lost. Zenocrate is made Queen of Persia, and as Tamburlaine is about to wed her, he announces that for her love he "takes truce with all the world." Her beauty and love have a great effect on him after all.

The precise relationship among beauty, love, and heroism was not clearly defined by Marlowe in the play, although it is evident that these are interdependent and mutually influential. Just as Zenocrate's beauty and love are appropriate attractions for Tamburlaine, his ferocity and invincibility seem equally appealing to her. And in some way that does not deny his warriorlike nature, Tamburlaine is made more compassionate and considerate by his love. His last-minute resolve to rule in peace may come as something of a surprise for a man of his disposition, but it comes as a logical resolution to the action, along with Tamburlaine's long-deferred marriage. Retirement may be hardly appropriate for this hero, but such a plan, however unsuited, is best delivered at the final curtain. Consistency of character, at least in the last minutes of the play, was not, it seems, an overriding concern of Marlowe's.

Tamburlaine's personality may ultimately lack coherence, but it does not fail in novelty. Defining the nature of man as restless, ambitious, and self-seeking rather than peaceful, charitable, and altruistic; emphasizing the notion that man is valued by his accomplishments rather than by his birth; reinterpreting the events of history as the results of individual will rather than the consequences of a divine master plan or an indifferent fortune—these are only three of the more radical attitudes expressed by the hero. And while the play celebrates the power, victories, and heroism of an historical ruler, it also portrays, albeit in positive terms, his cruelty, egotism, and tyranny. The form of the miracle play, the episodic narrative structure used to dramatize the life of Christ, is here adapted to relate the story of a secular figure whose life is anything but Christian.

No sensitive response to the play can be simple; approval of Tamburlaine's successes is encouraged by the attractiveness of his poetic speech; disapproval of his goals and tactics is aroused by the bloodiness of the action. Perhaps our squeamishness was not an

Elizabethan trait, but Marlowe was careful to sustain a mixed reaction. He studiously avoided dramatizing bloody encounters between his hero and his sympathetic characters; Tamburlaine, for example, does not himself slaughter innocent victims before our eyes. But the destruction and suffering that surround the protagonist are cause for disapprobation at the same time that his successes meet our applause. Having acknowledged the impurity of our emotion and the confusion of our ethics, we are left at the very end in amazement to admire and to celebrate the triumphant hero.

Tamburlaine the Great, PART II

The claim made in the prologue to *Tamburlaine the Great*, Part II, that the popularity of the first *Tamburlaine* play encouraged Marlowe to write a sequel, is probably true. Although the "two Tragicall discourses," the subtitle for *Tamburlaine the Great*, Parts I and II, were published together by Richard Jones in 1590 and never issued separately, there is nothing to suggest that Marlowe had the second in mind while writing the first. He scarcely seems to have remembered the earlier work while composing the later, for minor discrepancies and inconsistencies between the two parts, probably attributable to haste, forgetfulness, or indifference, abound.

In addition, had Marlowe actually planned two plays on the life of Tamburlaine from the outset, he might have apportioned his material differently. His two chief sources for the facts of Tamburlaine's career, Pedro Mexia's *Silva da varia lection* (1542), as it appeared in George Whetstone's *English Mirror* (1586), and Petrus Perondinus's *Magni Tamerlanis Scythiarum Imperatoria Vita* (1553), were used so prodigally in the first play that Marlowe left himself little new material with which to fill out the five acts of a second. As a consequence, he was forced to piece together diverse reading to make up Part II; accounts of the pact between Turks and Christians that led to the battle of Varna in 1444, the *Orlando Furioso*, and Paul Ive's *Practice of Fortification* (1589) were but a few.

An atlas, the *Theatrum Orbis Terrarum* (1570), drawn by the Renaissance cartographer Ortelius, was another important source of material in Part II.[1] Tamburlaine's campaigns through Asia and Africa were mapped out with precision by Marlowe, using Ortelius's atlas to plot the trail of his hero, and incorporating into his writing those place names that lend so much richness to his verse. Although Marlowe's geography may seem imaginary and fantastic, it is almost exclusively the product of careful study of one of the very best works of its kind then available. The Danube flows into the Mediterranean, and Zanzibar is on the west coast of Africa because that is, in fact, where Ortelius placed them.

Marlowe prepares the audience for Tamburlaine's entrance in Part II by reviewing his hero's accomplishments in the three opening scenes. Orcanes, King of Natolia, with his supporters, determines to sign a peace treaty with Christian Europe because Tamburlaine is marching toward his country with all the forces of Asia and Africa. The terms accepted by Turks and Christians are then ratified by formal oaths; Sigismund of Hungary vowing to Christ, Orcanes swearing "by sacred Mahomet."

In the third scene, Bajazeth's son, Callapine, a prisoner of Tamburlaine, successfully tempts his jailer, with promises expressed in language that could rival that of even Tamburlaine himself, to allow his escape.

> A thousand galleys, manned with Christian slaves,
> I freely give thee, which shall cut the Straits,
> And bring armadoes from the coasts of Spain,
> Fraughted with gold of rich America.
> The Grecian virgins shall attend on thee,
> Skillful in music and in amorous lays,
> As fair as was Pygmalion's ivory girl
> Or lovely Iö metamorphosèd.
> With naked negroes shall thy coach be drawn,
> And as thou rid'st in triumph through the streets,
> The pavement underneath thy chariot wheels
> With Turkey carpets shall be coverèd,
> And cloth of Arras hung about the walls,
> Fit objects for thy princely eye to pierce.

After such a speech it is not surprising that the jailer agrees to abandon Tamburlaine's service for Callipine's.

From his very first appearance it is evident that Tamburlaine will not always succeed in this play as he did in Part I. Zenocrate, his queen, is in ill health, and his concern for her is equaled only by his disappointment with his sons. Their delicacy of appearance and elegance of manner betray "their want of courage and of wit." And although two of his children deny their father's accusation of being "too dainty for the wars," the third, Calyphas, admits he would prefer to stay with his mother than take up arms.

Marlowe has quickly established in these opening scenes the united opposition of Tamburlaine's enemies, the treachery of one of Tamburlaine's own guards, and the extent of human frailty in his own home. The mood of this first act is far removed from the triumphant beginning of Part I, in which it would have been unthinkable for a soldier of Tamburlaine's to prove unfaithful, or in which it would have been incredible for an opponent to compete with his poetic or military prowess.

In the second act Sigismund, the Christian King of Hungary, is persuaded by religious pressure to break his pact with the Turks and attack their rear forces. The argument that is leveled against respecting the terms of the pact is highly specious: since pagans have proved untrustworthy, Christians should not be restricted by any agreements with them.

> But as the faith which they profanely plight
> Is not by necessary policy
> To be esteemed assurance for ourselves,
> So what we vow to them should not infringe
> Our liberty of arms and victory.

This reasoning is similar to what the Christian government uses as a rationale for its treatment of Jews and Turks in *The Jew of Malta*; the very word "policy," with its suggestion for the Elizabethans of Machiavellian statecraft, of Italian power politics, of self-seeking and self-serving decision making, betrays the real basis for the action. Although Sigismund rejects the argument, he permits his army, greatly outnumbering that of Orcanes, to be led against the Turks.

Orcanes calls on all heavenly powers, even challenging Christ to defend the Turks against the treachery of the Christians. The God of vitality and power he describes is rather like that restless and divine energy that Tamburlaine himself worships.

> That He that sits on high and never sleeps,
> Nor in one place is circumscriptible,
> But everywhere fills every continent
> With strange infusion of His sacred vigor,
> May, in His endless power and purity,
> Behold and venge this traitor's perjury!

And like Faustus in a later play, Orcanes does not realize that love and mercy are essential qualities of the Christian God.

The death of Sigismund in the battle and the Turkish victory that follows may be the result of divine retribution, but the very notion of a just, avenging God is denied by one of Orcanes's viceroys: " 'Tis but the fortune of the wars, my lord,/ Whose power is often proved a miracle." The Turkish success is as easily explained by an indifferent fortune as by a religious deity whose "miracles," it seems, are always suspect. And Marlowe casts doubt on the very existence of Christ by presenting Orcanes as a skeptic whose words are always carefully qualified by dependent clauses: "Then if there be a Christ, as Christians say," or "On Christ still let us cry,/ If there be Christ." The whole episode stresses the question not only of the trustworthiness of historians, but also of the possibility of God's involvement in man's affairs, and, indeed, the very existence of God.

The scene following the death of Sigismund and closing Act II dramatizes the death of Zenocrate. Sigismund's fall may be punishment for his sin, his "accursed and hateful perjury," but no causal connection is ever suggested linking Zenocrate's behavior and her dying. She sees her own death as simply a fact of the human condition, the result of those unalterable laws of nature that govern man indifferently.

> I fare, my lord, as other empresses,
> That, when this frail and transitory flesh
> Hath sucked the measure of that vital air
> That feeds the body with his dated health,
> Wane with enforced and necessary change.

Act III initiates those episodes that sustain the action through to its conclusion. Orcanes and Callapine will ultimately suffer defeat; Olympia, a distraught widow, will stab her son and frustrate the love of Tamburlaine's captain, Theridamas, by her suicide; and Tamburlaine will murder his youngest son for cowardice. Although much of this material is handled in a perfunctory manner, the many scenes of death and dying contribute to the dramatic spectacle.

In addition, through repetition and variation, death becomes a subject of thematic concern, culminating in the death of Tamburlaine himself at the very end of the play. Zenocrate dies with words about "dated health" and "enforced and necessary change," passing out of this life despite all her powerful husband and his court physicians can perform. Sigismund regarded his own demise as a "well-deserved" punishment for his treachery, but not all others think his death a direct result of divine intervention. For Olympia, suicide, long sought, is the fulfillment of her desires, reunion with her husband and child.

Tamburlaine's killing of his son Calyphas, very different from Olympia's murder of her son to spare him from Tamburlaine's soldiers, is almost a kind of ritual murder, eliminating a corrupted embodiment of his spirit. Calyphas, "created of the massy dregs of earth,/ The scum and tartar of the elements," is not fit as the progeny of the man who fathered him.

> Here, Jove, receive his fainting soul again,
> A form not meet to give that subject essence
> Whose matter is the flesh of Tamburlaine,
> Wherein an incorporeal spirit moves,
> Made of the mould whereof thyself consists.

In a very valuable study of Marlowe's intellectual development, Paul Kocher has pointed out that Tamburlaine's thinking, in this passage, strictly follows Renaissance Aristotelian logic: the soul of Calyphas is unworthy to be the immortal part of that body derived from the "flesh of Tamburlaine."[2] Tamburlaine thinks of himself as sharing in a kind of divine spirituality, an "essence" not to be tainted by Calyphas but to be passed on in equal portions to his two braver sons. They will inherit from him a spirit, proud and conquering like his own; they are the proper heirs of both the soul and body of their father.

Tamburlaine's increasing cruelty after the death of Zenocrate—razing the town in which she dies, murdering his son, hanging the governor of Babylon, slaughtering the inhabitants of that city—and his progressively more hysterical rhetoric may well be symptoms of insanity. Distraught over the loss of his queen, frustrated by his inability to control others or shape their lives to his satisfaction, Tamburlaine directs his strength and energy into accomplishments ever more savage and frenzied; his ferocity and madness are manifestations of what he describes as his "valiant, proud, ambitious" nature.

In the first scene of Act V, Tamburlaine performs his most defiant act. Challenging the power of Mahomet, he burns the Koran, "all the heaps of superstitious books . . . wherein the sum of thy religion rests." The "distemper" he feels almost immediately after the book burning is a sign of human frailty, and marks the onset of disease and death. The hero taunts Mahomet and even expresses some of Orcanes's skepticism: "The God that sits in heaven, if any god." But there is never open acknowledgment that his impending death is a direct consequence of blasphemy. That the destruction of the Koran is rapidly followed by the sickness of the hero suggests a causal relationship between these events, but there is none of the moralizing here that Orcanes, for example, offered over the death of Sigismund. Marlowe does not portray his hero explicitly as the victim of Mahomet. Tamburlaine repeatedly claims that he is the servant of a god decidedly more Christian, who "sits in heaven"

> full of revenging wrath,
> From whom the thunder and the lightning breaks,
> Whose scourge I am, and Him will I obey

Tamburlaine announces again and again that he is the "scourge of the immortal God," but it is difficult to determine the exact nature of what he worships, or of the role he casts for himself. His attitude is constantly changing. He compares himself to the gods, serves them, and expects either to join or conquer them; he defies them, obeys them, and thinks himself favored and abused by them. In short, his position is anything but consistent.

The phrase "scourge of God" suggests that Tamburlaine claims to derive his authority from a Christian deity, but, in the final analysis, there is no moral defense for his actions. Tamburlaine does as he pleases. He may argue that he implements divine will, but his actions certainly are not consistent with Christian notions of love, mercy, or justice. His god is a deity of naked power and ceaseless strife, the vital energy that he had described in Part I as the prime mover of the universe. And since Tamburlaine claims to derive his strength from Jove himself, he believes it is Jove who finally, "esteeming me too good for earth," would "mean t'invest me in a higher throne,/ As much too high for this disdainful earth." Tamburlaine thus reconciles himself and his sons to a greater will: "Nor bar thy mind that magnanimity,/ That nobly must admit necessity."

Again, as in Part I, Marlowe sustained an ambivalent attitude toward the moral outlook of the action. We admire and we are horrified as Tamburlaine is at the same time magnificent and appalling, possibly struck down by an angry god for blasphemy and possibly subsumed into the godhead itself at his final apotheosis in death.

> The scourge of God and terror of the world,
> I must apply myself to fit those terms,
> In war, in blood, in death, in cruelty,
> And plague such peasants as resist in me
> The power of heaven's eternal majesty.

Of impressive strength and control, Tamburlaine's language in Part II still occasionally matches the vaunting tones and rodomontade of Part I. Marlowe even extended the range of his poetry, at times achieving more moving and less flamboyant effects:

> See where my slave, the ugly monster Death,
> Shaking and quivering, pale and wan for fear,
> Stands aiming at me with his murdering dart,
> Who flies away at every glance I give,
> And when I look away, comes stealing on.

In his delirium the hero's imagination is more powerful here than in his description in the earlier play of that "imperious Death" who sits on the point of Tamburlaine's sword "keeping his circuit by the slicing edge."

On the whole, however, the poetry in Part II is less appealing. Marlowe's muse was flagging, and he substituted for blank verse of his own inspiration material more easily acquired, including, at the conclusion of Act IV, five lines from the first book of Spenser's *Fairie Queene*. It is also at the end of Act IV that Marlowe, who could turn out bombast as easily as some of his less talented contemporaries, wrote the most

famous example of heroic rant, Tamburlaine's entrance in a chariot drawn by captive kings. This passage was mocked on the English stage for years after-
ward; in fact, Shakespeare's Pistol, in *Henry IV*, Part
II, delivers the best-known parody of his braggadocio.

Although Marlowe's energies may not have been
as thoroughly involved in the production of this work,
although as a whole it may be less satisfying, there are
rare moments in Part II when his talents, fully engaged,
produce intense and moving results.

The earliest known record of a production of *Tamburlaine the Great* is a reference to events that take
place in Act V as they were described in a letter of 16
November 1587:

> You shall understand of some accidental news here
> in this town though my self no witness thereof,
> yet I may be bold to verify it for an assured truth.
> My Lord Admiral his men and players haveing a
> device in their play to tie one of their fellows to
> a post and so to shoot him to death, having bor-
> rowed them callivers, one of the players hands
> swerved, his piece being charged with bullet,
> missed the fellow he aimed at and killed a child,
> and a woman great with child forthwith, and
> hurt another man in the head very sore.[3]

According to Henslowe, the Admiral's Men in London performed Part I fifteen times and Part II seven
times between 28 August 1594 and 13 November
1595.[4] The plays were then, of course, not new, though
it must be assumed they were still enjoying popularity.
References to them are numerous, for they left a strong
impression on nearly every major playwright of the
Elizabethan-Jacobean period.

Although Henslowe also listed properties and costumes for mounting both plays in an inventory of

OPPOSITE: In a spectacular version that combined the two parts of Tamburlaine's history into a single evening, Tyrone Guthrie staged the first modern production of *Tamburlaine the Great* in 1951. Here Donald Wolfit portrays the dying hero as he surveys the world: "Give me a map; then let me see how much / Is left for me to conquer all the world."
RADIO TIMES HULTON PICTURE LIBRARY, LONDON

BELOW: In a scene that was mimicked by Renaissance playwrights for many years, Tamburlaine (Donald Wolfit) enters in a chariot drawn by captive kings.
RADIO TIMES HULTON PICTURE LIBRARY, LONDON

Eric Berry, as Barabas, buys a slave to serve as his tool
villain or henchman. The Royal Shakespeare Company
produced the *Jew of Malta* in Stratford-on-Avon and in
London in 1965.

ANTHONY CRICKMAY, LONDON

Feigning remorse and sorrow, Barabas (Eric Berry) laments his daughter's decision to enter a nunnery. To deceive the monks he proclaims his anguish in loud tones, while at the same time he reminds his daughter of their true plans in stage whispers.

ANTHONY CRICKMAY, LONDON

OPPOSITE: Ian McKellen, in the 1969 Prospect Theatre Company production of *Edward II*, at the Edinburgh Festival, was highly praised for his performance of Edward. The *New York Times* found that his acting, "controlled while passionate, induces pity and understanding for this weakest of kings."
PROSPECT PRODUCTIONS

BELOW: A defiant Gaveston, played by James Laurenson, is taken prisoner by the rebellious barons in the Prospect Theatre Company production.
PROSPECT PRODUCTIONS

OPPOSITE: Orson Welles, who considers this to have been the most rewarding of all his stage productions, starred in the Works Progress Administration version of *Doctor Faustus* in 1937. Highly influential and widely acclaimed, the play ran on Broadway for six months.
LINCOLN CENTER PERFORMING ARTS LIBRARY

BELOW: The Good and Bad Angels verbalize the fears and temptations in the divided mind of Faustus (Eric Berry) in the Royal Shakespeare Company production in Strat-ford-on-Avon.
LINCOLN CENTER PERFORMING ARTS LIBRARY

1598—"Tamberlyne brydell," "Tamberlanes breches of crymson vellvet," and "Tamberlaynes cotte with coper lace"—by the early years of the seventeenth century, the plays had dropped out of the repertory. Between the reopening of the theaters after the Puritan interregnum (1642–60) and the twentieth century, there is no record that the *Tamburlaine* plays were ever performed.

Since the turn of the century, amateur university productions of *Tamburlaine the Great* have been staged on both sides of the Atlantic. On the occasion of the four-hundredth anniversary of Marlowe's birth, the BBC arranged a radio production of both parts of *Tamburlaine*, with Stephen Murray in the title role.

The first recorded professional production since the early seventeenth century opened in London in 1951, when Tyrone Guthrie directed an abridged version of the two parts for the Old Vic. Donald Wolfit played Tamburlaine and Jill Bacon, Zenocrate. Guthrie then mounted the plays for the Shakespeare Festival of Stratford, Canada, and this production appeared at the Winter Garden Theater in New York in January 1956. It was an opportunity, wrote John Houseman (*New York Times*, 7 April 1974), "for some of his [Guthrie's] flashiest verbal and technical fireworks." Anthony Quayle played Tamburlaine, and Barbara Chilcott played Zenocrate. Reviewing the play in the *New York Times* (20 January 1956), Brooks Atkinson wrote: "Marlowe and Mr. Guthrie see eye to eye. They have collaborated on a horror play in strong blank verse and it is a triumphant theatre occasion."

The Jew of Malta

The Jew of Malta has none of the scope
and range of the *Tamburlaine* plays and little of their
exuberant dramatic poetry; it is, on initial contact,
perhaps less satisfying and less accessible than these.
In part, *The Jew of Malta* is less immediately ap-
proachable because Marlowe's attempt to portray complex characters is clumsily handled; in part, it is less
engaging because Marlowe's usually stirring language
is restrained in an effort to extend the range of blank
verse as a dramatic medium. Yet the work has an
appeal for modern audiences. *The Jew of Malta* shares
some of those characteristics of tone and action found
in contemporary theater: the touches of sardonic
cruelty and black humor; the mixture of melodrama
and farce.[1] And this play, with the most original of
Marlowe's plots, is less episodic than the Tamburlaine story. *The Jew of Malta* can be disappointing if
one expects to find in it another world conqueror, but
the drama is provocative and entertaining in its own
right.

Barabas, the titular character, is well-named, for like
his biblical namesake, who was freed in place of Christ,
he is a murderer and rebel. Before Barabas makes his

entrance on stage, however, a prologue announces that we are about to meet not a biblical character but a Renaissance man: Barabas is a Machiavel, a disciple of Niccolò Machiavelli.

The Elizabethan conception of a Machiavel owed little to the Florentine statesman whose political philosophy is expressed in *The Prince* and *The Discourses*, and more to the commentary on Machiavelli by Gentillet, a French Huguenot. In fact, first-hand knowledge of Machiavelli's writings was probably not widespread in Elizabethan England, where Gentillet's influence was pervasive. But even those who had some acquaintance with Machiavelli's work were shocked or, at least, they pretended to be. Machiavelli's realistic, pragmatic, and totally areligious discussion of *Realpolitik*, of the principles of expediency and force, of ends justifying means, of power and the ways of retaining it, were considered of hellish inspiration by more traditional Christian readers. To some degree, this reaction is understandable: the bare truths of the operations of government and of human psychology are often disturbing.

To prove conclusively the criminality and corruption of Machiavelli's theories, popular interpretation distorted and exaggerated his work. According to Gentillet's book, the *Contre-Machiavel* (1576), a Machiavel was one who practiced "policy," and this, simply defined, was the pursuit of any course of action, however immoral, that was self-advantageous. Murder, machinations, and deceit were all legitimate methods of achieving wealth, revenge, or supremacy. Religious or moral considerations were for the weak, foolish, or superstitious; such principles were hardly expected to deter the unscrupulous. Gentillet recognized two devices as the special trademark of a clever and experienced "politician": the use of a tool villain, a henchman employed to carry out the wishes of the Machiavel, who could later be charged with the deeds he was ordered to commit; and poisoning. To the Elizabethans the use of poison was thought an especially common Italian practice and, according to the *Contre-Machiavel*, was endorsed by Machiavelli himself.

Barabas, with his political chicanery, with his slave Ithamore, with his poisoned porridge and his deadly flowers, is a well-trained student of Italian politics. But it is only later in the play that the extent of his Machiavellianism becomes clear.

In the first scene of the play the Jew Barabas delivers three soliloquies, which emphasize primarily his wealth, his greed, and his egocentricity. To Barabas material prosperity is a consequence of heavenly favor. To be a member of the chosen people means for him, chosen to thrive; the answer to questions of honor or values is found in wealth. Power and rule—even government, so long as it is peacefully administered—interest him not at all. Barabas makes clear that he would reject "principality" were it offered, and, indeed, he does so in Act V. His one attachment is to his daughter, Abigail, "whom I hold as dear/ As Agamemnon did his Iphigen; / And all I have is hers." His comparison is appropriate, for he will later sacrifice her just as Agamemnon did Iphigenia. At the end of this first scene, Barabas delivers a brief restatement of his philosophy, in which his own interests and advantages are paramount: "How e'er the world go, I'll make sure for one."

There is an aspect of this opening scene that may be troubling. Barabas is the Machiavel, or so the prologue has informed us, but the key word "policy" is not applied to his methods at the beginning of the play.

When the word does appear twice in the first scene, it describes not Barabas's behavior, but rather that of the Turks; perhaps the Jew is not the only Machiavel here, but only the most infamous.

Despite the labeling, however, the Turks will prove less devious than either the Jews or the Christians. The Christian island of Malta, a tributary of the Turks, owes ten years' back taxes to the Turkish Sultan. As a "courtesy," Calymath, the Sultan's son, grants the Maltese governor, Ferneze, a month's extension to allow time for collecting the taxes. Acknowledging that " 'tis more kingly to obtain by peace/ Than to enforce conditions by constraint," Calymath warns Ferneze, "See you keep your promise."

To pay their national debt, Ferneze proposes to collect the tribute money for the Turks by taxing non-Christians exclusively. "Is theft the ground of your religion?" Barabas protests. But he is warned that if a man like him will not freely donate half his estate, he "shall absolutely lose all he has." Barabas does not readily accept the government's decree, and all his wealth is confiscated and his house converted to a nunnery.

> We take particularly thine
> To save the ruine of a multitude,
> And better one want for a common good
> Than many perish for a private man.

Ferneze's declaration is the same as that of every tyrant who has ever abrogated the state's responsibility for protecting individual rights; the "common good" is lost when freedom exists only at the whim of the magistrate. By contrast, Barabas makes his appeal to the highest law: "The man that dealeth righteously shall live,/ And which of you can charge me otherwise?" Furthermore, the constantly shifting grounds of the government's defense suggest the insecurity of its position: Barabas is cursed for his inherent sin; Barabas will regain his wealth if he is righteous; Barabas may be saved from the temptation of covetousness by his new poverty. One can sympathize with the Jew to whom none of this is very persuasive.

Spain also has a role in the power struggle over Malta, and hers is a complex one. Martin Del Bosco, the vice-admiral of Spain, who arrives on the island shortly after Calymath has left, warns Ferneze that his lord, the Catholic King of Spain, "hath title to this isle,/ And he means quickly to expel you hence." This threat and the suggestion that the Spanish king might be induced to change his mind are prompted by the 100,000 crowns of Turkish tribute money. Del Bosco proposes that Malta retain these taxes and turn to Spain for protection. His recommendation is not unreasonable. With such a treasury the King of Spain would find Malta attractive despite the Turkish claims, and a treaty between Catholic Malta and Catholic Spain would be more appropriate than the present agreement between the Maltese and the Turks. If their common religion did not provide enough of a bond, surely the wealth of Malta would appeal to Spanish interests; with military support expected from Spain, Ferneze feels powerful enough to refuse Calymath his payment.

Yet as it turns out, none of this holds true. Ferneze does break his word to the Turks, but in the war that follows in Act V, between the Turks and the Maltese, Spain offers no assistance to the island. She had not helped when "to Europe's shame" Rhodes was lost and "not a man survived/ To bring the hapless news to Christendom," nor will she risk war now with the Turks over Malta. Despite her claims, Spain serves her self-interest best by avoiding involvement in the affairs of the island. On a national level she practices the same philosophy Barabas has espoused.

Barabas, his riches confiscated by Ferneze, sets about swiftly regaining his lost wealth. In addition, with the help of Ithamore, a Turkish slave he has acquired, Barabas arranges for the death of Ferneze's son, a suitor for Abigail; when she turns against him, he poisons his daughter and the nunnery she enters after her suitor's death; and, because they know of his guilt, he strangles one friar and implicates another for the murder. Then, disguised as a French musician, Barabas eliminates Ithamore and his associates for blackmail and extortion.

Here is Barabas the Machiavel, with his tool villain and his poison. But Italian practices comprise only one aspect of his behavior. There is in his attitude and antics a kind of grotesque clowning, a frenzied and cruel humor that is older than any Renaissance influence. The *Contre-Machiavel* may have provided Marlowe with a new source for Barabas's philosophy and methodology, but the Vice figure of the morality plays was a prototype for Barabas's personality. The Vice, a kind of all-inclusive tempter acting for Satan, wittily and often obscenely succeeded in leading the morality play hero out of the paths of righteousness. He offered no reason for his wickedness; he was wicked by definition, and along with his unmotivated evil, he customarily took exceptional delight in his success. Barabas the Vice will even enjoy throwing away some of his money for the sake of wicked deeds, although this is incompatible with his miserliness.

> As for myself, I walk abroad 'a nights
> And kill sick people groaning under walls.
> Sometimes I go about and poison wells,

And now and then, to cherish Christian thieves,
I am content to lose some of my crowns
That I may, walking in my gallery,
See 'em go pinioned along by my door.

It is because of this very mixed parentage that Barabas's behavior is occasionally confusing, his motivation inconsistent, and the tone of the play sometimes jarring. The different philosophies and literary influences are not well blended. The actions of Marlowe's crafty Machiavel are not always consistent with the antics of a bustling buffoon, complete with putty nose, who delights in his own capacity for evil like the Vice, the unmotivated devil figure of earlier drama. Nevertheless, despite Marlowe's failure to combine the Vice character and the popular notion of an Italian statesman into a cohesive personality, the Jew of Malta is a commanding and theatrically exciting figure.

In the first scene of Act V, his crimes revealed to Ferneze by his dying victims, Barabas feigns death to escape punishment. He is cast over the walls of the city, discovered by Calymath, and agrees to aid the Turks in taking over Malta. This accomplished, Calymath, "as erst we promised thee," places Barabas in charge of the island and of his Christian prisoners. Since Barabas's policy, however, is not to accrue power of position but wealth, he bargains with the captive Ferneze to overthrow the Turks for "great sums of money." This time his plan fails, for at the end of the play Ferneze allows Barabas to fall into the boiling cauldron that the Jew had prepared for Calymath. The Christians regain control of the island and take Calymath as their hostage.

Ferneze here demonstrates his dishonesty once again. As he had broken his vow to pay the Turks, so he breaks his word to Barabas. Ferneze is, after all, politic.

He succeeds ultimately in ridding his country of both the oppressive Turks and the wicked Jew, and for this he is surely to be applauded. But what is at issue is the difficulty of reconciling Ferneze's tactics with Christian ethics: he represents Catholic principles of conduct, yet his actions are of very questionable morality.

Marlowe's occasional gibes at Catholics here and elsewhere were nothing more than shooting at fair game; nuns and monks, after all, were usual subjects for Protestant low comedy. What is unusual, is the portrayal of a Christian governor who wins by outfoxing Machiavels through Machiavellian duplicity. Perhaps one can argue sophistically that it is not sinful to break a promise to a heathen in a Christian cause; Barabas himself cites the axiom: "Faith is not to be held with heretics." Such reasoning may be offered as an excuse, but Ferneze is nevertheless left a character without nobility or stature.

Barabas's description of Christianity as the ethic of "malice, falsehood, and excessive pride" is not unjustified in this play; the Christians are unreliable in their word. The Turks, however, are not, allowing the Maltese a month's extension and rewarding Barabas as promised with the governorship. In every way Calymath acts with honesty and sincerity. He and his bashaws are the most removed from the tradition that has shaped the morality of the Christians and Jews of Malta, yet judged by that morality, they are certainly the most truthful, trustworthy, and courteous. They, it seems, are more truly "Christian" than either Christians or Jews.

Nevertheless, in the world of *The Jew of Malta*, altruism, self-sacrifice, and forgiveness are meaningless terms to all men, with no bearing on behavior. Self-interest and greed dominate men's lives in a world without spiritual values, a world in which materialism rules:

FERNEZE: What wind drives you thus into Malta road?

BASHAW: The wind that bloweth all the world besides,
Desire of gold.

In such a world Barabas is only one among the wicked. Our response to the action of the play can be neither unambiguous nor simple.

Marlowe's manipulation of his dramatic and thematic material is further complicated by his blank verse, for Marlowe the playwright was not always in control of Marlowe the poet. The complexity of the theme is not always appropriately conveyed by the writing. There are sudden shifts in language and mood, due either to aspects of character that have resisted integration into a unified stage personality, or to indulgence in headier kinds of lyricism. With his first words in the play Barabas reveals a familiar delight in language. Like Tamburlaine he can deliver catalogues of proper nouns:

Bags of fiery opals, sapphires, amethysts,
Jacinths, hard topaz, grass-green emeralds,
Beauteous rubies, sparkling diamonds,
And seld-seen costly stones

He can offer aphoristic or epigrammatic pronouncements:

And thus methinks should men of judgment frame
Their means of traffic from the vulgar trade,
And as their wealth increaseth, so enclose
Infinite riches in a little room.

Or he can put together phrases rich in assonance and alliteration:

> Mine argosy from Alexandria,
> Loaden with spices and silks, now under sail,
> Are smoothly gliding down by Candy shore
> To Malta, through the Mediterranean sea.

All of these excerpts are from one speech, which, offered whole, is typical of the language Marlowe wrote for his vaunting heroes. Though such a soliloquy is exhilarating, the speaker is not exactly suited to its delivery: Barabas is not, after all, so much world-conqueror as clown.

Often the tone of the play, too, changes radically. The love scene of Ithamore, Barabas's slave, and Bellamira, a courtesan, is a grotesquely humorous exaggeration, a deliberate debasing of Ovidian poetic conventions and of pastoral idealization by two of the least romantic or attractive characters in world drama.[2] And for Ithamore to end his tirade with the words "live with me, and by my love" makes the speech a kind of burlesque of the well-known lyrics of Marlowe's "Passionate Shepherd."

Marlowe, more talented than disciplined, enjoyed demonstrating his versatility. As has already been shown, soliloquies and set pieces in this play are sometimes ends in themselves, passages of verbal dexterity, humor, or experimentation that do not serve the main purposes of the drama but are instead a kind of splendid self-indulgence by Marlowe. This weakness, also present in the *Tamburlaine* plays, seems more pervasive in *The Jew of Malta* because here neither the protagonist nor the theme lends itself readily to flights of blank-verse exuberance. Yet, Marlowe was working to develop a form of verse dialogue capable of carrying forward the plot in the less exciting or exaggerated moments of drama. Del Bosco's account of his en-counter with the Turks in Act II is a good example of this highly adaptable writing.

> Because we vailed not to the Turkish fleet,
> Their creeping galleys had us in the chase;
> But suddenly the wind began to rise,
> And then we luffed and tacked and fought at ease.
> Some have we fired and many have we sunk.

Del Bosco's narrative handles the necessary exposi-tion briefly but with attention to detail. Marlowe's verbs suggest strenuous movement and energy as well as naval maneuvering. The three verbs "luffed and tacked and fought," convey the frenzy of battle. The motion and speed of the attacking Turkish ships is contrasted with the agility of the Spanish galleons, which turn on them when the wind rises. The Spanish fleet seems to have greater mobility because Marlowe has increased the number of verbs and used mono-syllabic words exclusively to describe them. Finally, with strictly balanced clauses, the last line summarizes the retelling and leads into the conclusion: "Some have we fired and many have we sunk."

Although *The Jew of Malta* is the least popular of Marlowe's maturer works, its importance in his de-velopment cannot be overstated. It lacks consistency of character and tone; it does not display the dramatist in full control of his powers. But in intricacy of plotting, in adaptability and range of verse, in versatility of character and in complexity of theme, the play is highly sophisticated. And what is more, Marlowe accomplished all of this without sacrificing those ele-ments of violent stage action that the Elizabethans expected in their theater.

Henslowe did not indicate a first performance of *The Jew of Malta* in his *Diary*, but the frequency of entries, the size of the receipts, and the number of acting companies that performed the play attest to its great popularity. From February 1592 to June 1596, it is mentioned thirty-six times, and in May 1601, Henslowe evidently planned a revival, for he spent five pounds "to bye divers things for the Jewe of Malta" and paid ten shillings "more to the littell tayller the same daye for more things for the Jewe of malta."[3]

The play received alterations when Thomas Heywood prepared a prologue and an epilogue for the performances given at court and at the Cock Pit Theatre; Heywood may also have tampered with the text. The 1633 quarto, the only extant version of the work, was printed from a manuscript prepared by Heywood.

There is no indication that Barabas appeared on a stage in the eighteenth century. A production of the play was mounted, in a new version prepared by Edmund Kean, in 1818. The work was revived by Williams College, in Williamstown, Massachusetts, in 1907, by the Phoenix Society in London in 1922, and by the Yale Dramatic Association in 1940.

The most recent professional production of *The Jew of Malta* was staged in repertory, with Shakespeare's *The Merchant of Venice*, by the Royal Shakespeare Company in London and Stratford-on-Avon in 1965. Eric Berry portrayed both Barabas and Shylock. The *New York Times* wrote that "the plays are a tour de force for Mr. Berry, who plays the Marlowe role expansively for laughs. . . . One feels at the end of *The Jew of Malta* that there has been no tragedy but a coruscating burlesque."

The Massacre at Paris

The study of Marlowe's *Massacre at Paris* is complicated by the state of the printed text. Its great brevity, its excessive repetition of phrases and lines, its garbled blank verse, and its failure to offer as complete a version of some of the dialogue as an extant manuscript fragment—all constitute strong evidence that the printed edition is a "bad" quarto of Marlowe's original work, a quarto probably patched together by a few actors who relied on their own imperfect memories to reconstruct Marlowe's lines.[1] The actors would naturally reproduce their own roles with greater accuracy and record scenes during which they were on stage with more assurance than others. But even after acknowledging variations in the quality of the text, one finds the level of the speeches and of the characterization here generally inferior to anything else by Marlowe.

Since, in its debased condition, *The Massacre at Paris* probably offers only a faint impression of Marlowe's original handling of plot, of theme, and, at least with the central figure, of character, it would be unrewarding to examine this work in great detail. Marlowe dramatized the cruelty and wickedness of the French Catholics, led by the Duke of Guise and the Queen Mother, Catherine de Medici, in their persecution of the innocent Huguenots. The source for the first half of this play, *A true and plaine report of the Furious outrages of Fraunce* (1573), was supplemented by other accounts that cover the period between the massacre on St. Bartholomew's Day, in 1572, and the murder of the Guise in 1588 and Henry III in 1589. Marlowe may have even known firsthand something about English priests trained "at Rheims/ To hatch forth treason 'gainst their natural queen," for in 1587, the Privy Council, intervening with Cambridge on Marlowe's behalf, acknowledged that he was reported "to have gone beyond the seas to Reames and there to remaine."

The play is overwhelmingly in sympathy with the Huguenots, but then no playwright would or could have done otherwise in Elizabethan England. Apart from the possibility of personal involvement, the historical facts and the personalities of the principal Frenchmen would surely have interested Marlowe. His concern with the machinations of power politics, his fascination with dominating personalities like the Guise, and his readiness to capitalize commercially on events that deeply concerned Englishmen would have been sufficient to attract him to this story.

The Massacre at Paris has, in fact, much in common with Marlowe's other works. The pride, self-assurance, and fierceness of the Guise are attributes he shares with Tamburlaine, who also thought that a crown was the highest goal of all. In cruelty and villainy, however, the Guise is more like Barabas, though perhaps less conscious of the influence of Machiavelli. Marlowe organized the events of the play in a rather simple and straightforward manner, less confusing than the conflict in *The Jew of Malta* and less sophisticated than what was to be attempted in *Edward II*. In fact, *The Jew of Malta* may have been written immediately before and *Edward II* immediately after *The Massacre at Paris*.

Marlowe seems to have determined to exploit the notoriety of his material in two ways. First the events themselves provide moments of violent and bloody action for which there was strong audience taste; these Marlowe dramatized with relish. Second, the widespread familiarity in London with the recent course of events in France allowed Marlowe to stress the irony in his material by juxtaposing the words of his characters against their deeds, pointing up the opposition between them. It is exactly this pattern that provides the organizing principle throughout.

The play opens with the marriage of the sister of the Catholic King of France, Charles IX, to the King of Navarre, a Protestant. Both men express the hope that this union will assure a league of peace between their religions. The irony of these sentiments is stressed in the very next scene when the Guise, using religion as a cover for his own ambition to gain the throne, exposes in soliloquy his plans for murdering both Navarre's mother and the Protestant Admiral Coligny. The Guise is not successful immediately—Coligny is wounded but not killed in the third scene—but he and Catherine de Medici persuade Charles reluctantly to leave matters entirely in their hands. The Guise reveals to them his arrangements for a Protestant massacre. To continue his pretense that all is well, Charles falsely reassures Coligny and Navarre of his continued support.

The massacre of St. Bartholomew's Day follows,

presented in a series of bitterly humorous vignettes. The logician Ramus, for example, is murdered as conclusive proof of the refutation of his logic. The slaughter of the Protestants seems to end with the sudden death of Charles; his fate, he suggests as he is dying, is a consequence of his perfidy. His brother, the Duke of Anjou, is named to the throne as Henry III, and Navarre, until now a passive and ineffectual hero, leaves Paris for his home territory.

The main thrust of the remaining action concerns the antagonism between the new king and the Guise, rather than the hatred of the Catholics for the Protestant minority. Catherine de Medici and the Guise expect that the new king, Henry III, will indulge himself with his minions while they continue their extermination of religious opposition. Their plans are disrupted, however, when the Guise discovers his wife's love affair with Mugeroun, one of Henry's friends. Insulted as a cuckold, the Guise arranges for the assassination of Mugeroun. Henry then attempts to limit the power of the Guise, ordering the dismissal of his private army. Failing that, he manages the murder of the Guise at Blois. To insure his security further, Henry orders the elimination of the Guise's two brothers. One of these, the Cardinal of Lorraine, is strangled; but the other, the Duke Dumaine, escapes and, with a friar, plots to kill the king.

In this half of the play, the conflict between the crown and the Guise is interspersed with brief segments involving the war of the Protestants against the Catholic armies and Navarre's victory over the French military leader, the Duke Joyeux. Finally, the last scene of the play dramatizes the new peace agreement between Henry III and Navarre, the stabbing of Henry by the friar, his dying warning to Elizabeth in England,

and the ascending of Navarre to the crown of France.

Everywhere the irony is stressed and often in a heavy-handed manner: the audience knows, despite the claims of the dialogue, that the marriage of a Catholic princess and a Protestant king will not end the hatred between their religions; the audience knows, despite his claims, that Henry III is wrong to think no friar need be searched before being admitted to see him: "Our friars are holy men/ And will not offer violence to their King/ For all the wealth and treasure of the world." Finally, an English audience in 1594, only a year after Navarre decided Paris was worth a mass, would have appreciated the irony—this time, unintended by Marlowe—of Navarre's closing lines:

> And then I vow for to revenge his death
> As Rome and all those popish prelates there
> Shall curse the time that e'er Navarre was King
> And rul'd in France by Henry's fatal death.

Navarre and the Guise are the two principal figures. The Protestant leader is a disappointing hero. His characterization may owe its pallor to the debasement of the text, which might have damaged his role more than others; and in addition, the historical irony of Navarre's conversion to Catholicism in July 1593, a month after the death of Marlowe, may have made a readjustment of Marlowe's portrait necessary. If the quarto, published probably in the early 1600s, reflects the acting version of the play after 1593, the role of Navarre may well have been altered to present him as a less idealized image of the Protestant king to whom the English had been sending money and arms.

The character of the Guise, on the other hand, is much in the vein of those other Marlowe creations who "go as whirlwinds rage before a storm." Indeed, his is the soul of a Machiavel, or so the prologue to *The Jew of Malta* explains. Barabas, in that play, is a reincarnation of Machiavelli through the Guise:

Albeit the world think Machiavel is dead,
Yet was his soul but flown beyond the Alps,
And, now the Guise is dead, is come from France
To view this land and frolic with his friends.

In a long set speech in the second scene of *The Massacre at Paris*, the Guise defines his personality and most fully describes his philosophy. Of an ambitious nature, striving incessantly, loving danger, desiring greatness even at the risk of damnation—the Guise shares these attributes with other Marlovian characters. "What glory is there in a common good," he asks, finding attractive only enterprises that are extraordinary for their difficulty. The Guise admits that religion itself is not an issue. But, by feigning a sincere devotion to the Catholic cause, he intends to shape a policy that will lead him to the throne of France. Religion is only a cover, "a word of such a simple sound" that it alone could never be the real motive for his actions.

The Guise considers the actual political situation in France, the irresponsibility of King Charles, the devotion of Catherine—"Rifling the bowels of her treasury,/ To supply my wants and necessity"—and his support in the colleges and religious institutions of Paris. Renewing his intention to seize the crown and rejecting the threat of the "petty king" Navarre, he restates in a peroration his resolution to rule the country.

Give me a look that, when I bend the brows,
Pale death may walk in furrows of my face;
A hand that with a grasp may gripe the world;

An ear to hear what my detractors say;
A royal seat, a sceptre, and a crown;
That those which do behold, they may become
As men that stand and gaze against the sun.

The continuation of the thought over several lines suspending the verse period, the careful alliteration (bend, brows; furrows, face; grasp, gripe; seat, sceptre), the smooth transition from brows to face, from face to hand, from hand to ear, are examples of admirable blank-verse writing. Marlowe avoids the stiffness that would result from rigid parallelism; the three nouns in succession, "A royal seat, a sceptre, and a throne," bring weight and finality to the restatement of the Guise's ambition, the crown of France itself; and the last two lines reverse the point of view: rather than describing the qualities of the Guise, they express the reactions of those who approach a man with his qualities. Although this is not a blank-verse passage of great distinction, it is, nevertheless, highly successful dramatic poetry, carrying forward the action and developing the character and the intrigue with spirit and feeling.

The Massacre at Paris may prove ultimately disappointing, but one should remember that the ease, the fluidity, the control of movement and expression occasionally found here were skills rarely displayed by Marlowe's contemporaries in the 1580s.

The first receipts, exceptionally high, noted by Henslowe in his *Diary* for *The Massacre of Paris* was for a production by Lord Strange's Men of "the tragedey of the gvyes," in January 1593. This was probably the first performance of the work.[2] Shortly after this, the theaters closed because of a plague epidemic. Henslowe next recorded a performance of a

"Gwies," in June 1594, and, nine times over the next four months, of a work called "the masacer."[3] Since receipts for all these productions show a steady and proportionate decline, it is a fairly safe assumption that Henslowe was referring to the same play by these different titles.

A revival of the work may have been planned in 1598, for Henslowe lent money to one actor "to Imbrader his hatte for the gwisse" and to another "to bye a payer of sylke stockens to playe the gwisse in."[4] A second refurbishing evidently took place in November 1601, when Henslowe again financed the expenses for "stamell cllath for A clocke for the gwisse," and supplied the Admiral's Men with the cash "to lend the littell tayller to bye fuschen and lynynge for the clockes for the masaker of france."[5] His *Diary*'s final entry for the play, on 12 January 1602, concerns payment to Edward Alleyn for the purchase of this and three other plays for the Admiral's Men.[6]

Two productions of the play in the 1900s deserve note. Three performances were staged by the Yale Dramatic Association in the fall of 1940, and, in 1972, Roger Planchon opened the new Théâtre National Populaire in Villeurbanne (Lyons), France, with a loosely adapted version of Marlowe's *Massacre at Paris* by Jean Vauthier.

Doctor Faustus

Doctor Faustus is superficially very much like the *Tamburlaine* plays and *The Jew of Malta.* All three have for their protagonists men of power and daring, men whose very natures drive them to exceed the restrictions of their society. All three plays are episodic to a degree, and each ends with the death of the central character. The climax of each of these works is ambiguous because on the one hand, the sense of order necessary for society to continue, a simple justice in the grain of things, demands that the Marlovian protagonist meet disaster; on the other hand, the catastrophe brings with it feelings of admiration, of wonder at the strength and capability displayed by the central figure. In comparison to him, all else seems of questionable value, contemptible and petty.

Doctor Faustus differs, however, from these earlier plays in two important respects. Tamburlaine and Barabas measure success by material prosperity; possessing an "earthly crown" is "sweet fruition" for the world conqueror; gathering "infinite riches" is the most satisfying endeavor for the Jew. But Faustus's desires are intangible; crowns and coins, lands and wealth are far from the center of his interests. His monomania is to know all, for in his judgment such knowledge is the supreme form of power. Faustus, in short, would reenact the sin of Satan; he would himself become a god. This sophistication in the hero's ambition demanded a character of greater depth and subtlety. Accordingly, Marlowe attempted to use his dramatic poetry for the expression of a psychological state of mind. The central conflict in this play is not between the title character and his society, but within the mind of Faustus himself. The dramatic and musical qualities of Marlovian blank verse are here directed to spiritual and ethical issues, to those larger questions involving the motivation of a complex personality.

Marlowe closely followed an English translation of a German *Faustbuch*, *The Historie of the Damnable Life and Deserved Death of Doctor John Faustus*, which had appeared in London by 1592. From this Marlowe took the main outlines of his plot, the tale of a man who signs a contract with Lucifer, who passes his years exercising magic powers, and who finally dies unredeemed. Damned for the practice of necromancy, the hero of the *Faustbuch* performs almost all the actions of the hero of the play; even many of the play's scenes of low comedy originated there.

Marlowe assumed responsibility for the main shape and treatment of the plot; in all likelihood a collaborator (or collaborators) supplied the prose farce scenes and some of the heavy-handed blank-verse writing. Samuel Rowley, an actor and author with the Admiral's Men, is most often thought to have penned these. The study of Marlowe's *Doctor Faustus* is complicated, however, not only because the text was probably a collaborative effort, but also because the popularity and longevity of the work on the stage may well have contributed to the debasing of Marlowe's material before it found its way into print.[1] In fact, the early printed editions of the play differ radically. Any attempt to establish now a version as close as possible to that written originally must therefore involve a degree of speculation.

Despite the adulteration and corruption of Marlowe's drama, however, its main outline remains distinct enough to reveal a work of extraordinary power, beauty, and intelligence. The writing of Shakespeare apart, Marlowe's Faustus is, perhaps, the most imposing tragic hero in English literature and one of the archetypal figures of Western civilization. What Marlowe accomplished in his organization and treatment of the story of the wonderworking doctor could not have been found in any source material. Most impressive in his handling is the manner in which he has shaped his material to dramatize the effects of guilt and anguish on a sensitive and perceptive intellect. Capitalizing on the audience's knowledge of Faustus's fate, Marlowe made effective use of dramatic irony. Exploring the connection between pact and deed, he traced the steady degeneration of the hero, the waste, the loss, the suffering involved as Faustus voluntarily acts out a life that will prove finally unsalvable. As Goethe is reported to have said when he read it, "How greatly is it all planned!"

The strength of the play rests largely in Marlowe's control over his blank verse, in the greater range and intensity of emotions his poetry conveys. More than in his earlier plays, Marlowe was capable here of communicating the sensations of experience and at the same time of commenting on the effects of these experiences. As a poet, he revealed here an extraordinary power of expression, so that a brief passage can easily display, along with those elements most characteristic of his style, his fondness for the sounds of proper names or exotic vocabulary, his creative use of his classical education, and his awareness of contemporary history and politics. In *Doctor Faustus*, Marlowe's verse has become a supple instrument immediately responsive to a variety of moods and a wide range of ideas.

Doctor Faustus opens with a chorus speech that sets the stage. The subject now is neither war nor love; the poetry will sing not of "proud audacious deeds" but rather the "form of Faustus' fortunes, good or bad." That is, we must expect to see not the fortunes themselves, but the overall effect of those fortunes, for, as C. L. Barber has noted, action becomes a kind of Platonic symbolism, an intellectualizing of experience.[2] The chorus also establishes a central image or pattern for the action. Through the language of gormandizing, of consuming or devouring, the insatiability of Faustus's drive finds expression; he is "swollen" or distended with knowledge; "glutted" with learning, he "surfeits" upon black magic.

In the soliloquy that follows, Faustus voices his discontent with the state of his knowledge. Having mastered the curriculum of the medieval university, he finds himself, in the best liberal arts tradition, ill-prepared for life. Philosophy is good only for disputation; medicine, unable to grant eternal life or raise the dead, is useful only for money and fame; law, too, "servile and illiberal," is best only for "a mercenary drudge." Finally, theology, the queen of the sciences, is reduced by him to a doctrine of fatalism, "Che sera, sera." He bases this fatalism on a quotation from the first epistle of St. John: "If we say that we have no sin, we deceive ourselves, and the truth is not in us."

The syllogism Faustus constructs from this statement is quite simple: man must sin; the reward of sin is death; man must die "an everlasting death." The human condition must then lead inevitably to eternal damnation.

But Faustus is better at logic than he is at theology, for his interpretation of this passage is valid only if one disregards the next line in the epistle: "If we confess our sins, He is faithful and just to forgive us our sins, and to cleanse us from all unrighteousness." Faustus acknowledges that man is condemned by the letter of the law, but he does not realize that through faith, repentance, and the sacrifice of Christ man can be redeemed.

Perhaps there is a connection to be made between Faustus's theology and the setting of the play, for Wittenberg is also the city where Luther nailed his theses to the door of the cathedral, a city closely identified with the Reformation and the Protestant movement. Although a thorough comprehension of Protestant belief is not essential to an understanding of *Doctor Faustus*, some of the more distinctly non-Catholic practices of the new faith may well have affected the play. The severity and remoteness of Faustus's conception of God, for example, may reflect, in part, the prohibition of the practice of auricular confession and the denial of the role of the saints as intercessors. The Protestant sinner or penitent now addressed God directly himself. Though some may have thought communication vastly improved, others, no doubt, found the distance between them and their God greatly increased. A priest granting absolution and a panoply of saints offering spiritual support were, for some, comforts of Catholicism that found no replacement in Protestantism. Furthermore, Luther's

Protestantism, proclaiming justification by faith alone, would be disturbing to those who had placed value in works and deeds. And Calvin's Protestantism, claiming all men are born either Elect or Damned, denied the existence of purgatory, the possibility of achieving salvation at some time after death. Faustus could not expect that heaven would "impose some end to my incessant pain."

All of this is not to argue that Marlowe's play is pro-Catholic, or anti-Protestant. It would be a serious distortion and simplification of the work to reduce it to a piece of religious or political propaganda. *Doctor Faustus* should be considered Marlowe's expression of those unresolved, persistently disquieting emotions that trouble all men and that were especially disturbing to Renaissance Englishmen because of the religious controversy in the sixteenth century. His country, after all, had shifted from Catholicism to Protestantism three times within the century, and the future of the Church of England was hardly secure with the unmarried, aging Queen Elizabeth on the throne. Marlowe created drama, then, out of a controversial issue, but not out of an urge to settle such questions— if, indeed, they can be settled.

In his soliloquy, Faustus, having rejected theology, remarks that his "necromantic books are heavenly." Surely, in one sense, that adjective is misplaced here; it is clear that Faustus's new curriculum is forbidden fruit and that the consequences of his actions will condemn him. But Marlowe has chosen his words carefully, for Faustus by his very language devalues his new course of study even before he undertakes it. Marlowe repeatedly employs dramatic irony, writing lines that carry one meaning for Faustus but another for the audience. Since, in fact, Faustus has said,

"Divinity adieu!" it is ironic that Marlowe has Faustus call his new subject "heavenly." It was theology that was unsatisfying, and it is in opposition to divinity that he turns to profane studies. With his description of black magic as "heavenly," Faustus has discounted his newest source of knowledge in advance, pointing up its inability to prove ultimately rewarding.[3]

After this soliloquy the Good and Bad Angels make their first appearance. Such one-dimensional, allegorical characters would be more at home in morality plays, a genre that, although still performed in the last half of the sixteenth century, was old-fashioned by the 1590s. These figures, however, are not personifications of forces outside of man so much as the conflicting forces within him, the Good Angel warning of God's "heavy wrath," and the Bad Angel extolling the power of magic. For Marlowe's purposes, the angels are a dramatic, if somewhat clumsy, device primarily for verbalizing the struggle that is being played out within the mind of the hero.

Here, again, Marlowe was being subtly ironic. Allegorical characters, spokesmen for heaven and hell, would suggest to Marlowe's audience the format of the traditional morality drama in which an Everyman figure, tempted by evil in some form, succumbs, repents, and finally is saved. The point of such works is that divine mercy is inexhaustible, that heaven is of infinite compassion. No sin is unforgivable. Marlowe mixed the standard ingredients by the set formula, but he created a totally new product. With Faustus cast as Everyman, with the devices of the morality play scattered throughout the action, his drama ends not with the expected salvation of the hero but with his final torment and damnation.

After the Angels leave him, the wonders of magic

are praised by Faustus, thrilled by the prospects of his future power. Again, verbs of eating are used to describe his ambition: he is "glutted" with imagining, his mind "ruminates" only on black magic. Faustus takes his teachers in to dine after they have considered how their efforts will make him "blessed" or how their "experience/ Shall make all nations to canonize us." The religious terminology deliberately and ironically contradicts the context in which it is placed. When Faustus remarks, "Oh this cheers my soul!" Marlowe implies the opposite meaning.

The low comedy scene that follows, like all the humorous scenes of *Doctor Faustus* at their best, was intended to reflect the serious action; at their worst they were meant to satisfy a popular taste for horseplay and clowning. When Faustus's servant Wagner, asked by two scholars where his master is, answers that "God in heaven knows," the reply directs attention to the course Faustus has just chosen. When Wagner indulges in a kind of choplogic, he is mimicking the logic-chopping of a master who can build a case on one sentence in the Bible but ignore the qualifying remarks that immediately follow it.

Such deliberate distortion of fact is practiced by Faustus again in the very next scene, when Mephistophilis first appears. Faustus claims that Mephistophilis was drawn to him by magic; Mephistophilis announces that he came "of mine own accord." Faustus persuades himself that he can "command great Mephistophilis"; but Mephistophilis tells Faustus that he is "servant to great Lucifer." Faustus boasts that the "word 'damnation' terrifies not me"; Mephistophilis confesses that he himself is "tormented with ten thousand hells." When, finally, Faustus sounds arrogant and disdainful, "Learn thou of Faustus manly fortitude

/ And scorn those joys thou never shalt possess," Mephistophilis reminds us that Lucifer, too, was thrown from heaven "for aspiring pride and insolence."

Faustus's ability to conjure Mephistophilis cannot, after all, have been a skill so difficult to acquire since it is displayed by Wagner in the very next scene. This little comic interlude reduces the magnificence of Faustus's courage to foolish willfulness. Although Faustus agrees to bind himself to Lucifer after twenty-four years, Robin, a hungry clown, knows better than to "give his soul to the devil for a shoulder of mutton." Should the clown, however, not bind himself to Wagner for seven years, Wagner threatens to turn lice into familiars "and make them tear thee in pieces." Indeed, Faustus learns the devil has such power. For Faustus to "be great emperor of the world," on the one hand, or for the clown "to turn . . . into a dog or a cat, or a mouse, or a rat, or anything," on the other, is only a difference of degree, not of kind.

As he signs his soul over to Lucifer, in the first scene of Act II, Faustus realizes that "the God thou serv'st is thine own appetite." For him to seal his bargain with "*Consummatum est*," quoting the words of the dying Savior, appropriately contrasts the supreme example of self-sacrifice with the supreme example of self-indulgence.

Once the contract is sealed Faustus is seized by increasing fear and insecurity. He will constantly need to remind himself to be "resolute." Mephistophilis knows that the scholar will always require "somewhat to delight his mind." Dancing devils, the first entertainment in what will become a lifetime of distractions, present Faustus crowns and clothes.

The drives that motivate Faustus, the appetites that he tries to satisfy, are sensual as well as intellectual, for

Faustus not only delights in music but also longs for marriage. Having just sold his soul for power and experience, Faustus learns, ironically, that his very first demand is unattainable: Mephistophilis cannot fulfill his request for a wife. Marriage is a sacrament that cannot be administered by hell to the damned; but a "hot whore indeed," "the fairest courtesans," whomever Faustus chooses, however chaste, or wise, or fair, can be brought to his bed by Mephistophilis. The implication here is that Faustus will always choose someone as corruptible as he is himself, as corruptible "as was bright Lucifer before the fall." Mephistophilis is simply suggesting that like attracts like; Goethe's Gretchen would never have appealed to Marlowe's Faustus.

As Faustus was denied complete satisfaction in his sensual appetite, so his intellectual desires also remain frustrated. He learns answers only to the less complex problems, the "slender questions." He cannot be taught, for example, who made the world. His interests, as they develop after his pact with Lucifer, shift from the earlier involvement with fundamental and philosophic concerns, from cosmic and metaphysical problems, to shallower and narrower fields of study. The astronomy of Act II gives way to the cosmography of Act III, and the ambitions of the intellectual soon become the adventures of the merely curious. The man who was first characterized by his restless and questioning mind soon appears merely a dilettante seeking novelty and amusement. And when curiosity is itself sated, only the desire for entertainment and diversion remains.

Acts III and IV are a disappointment after the excitement of the poetry and action of the opening; the intensity of the first two acts is not sustained. Even

allowing for Marlowe's slighter interest or involvement in the comic scenes that occupy the stage during
this middle section of the play, the level of the writing
and the development of plot and theme are not satisfying. The action here is divided roughly between two
levels of society: one with characters of political or
social status such as Bruno and the Pope, Emperor
Charles V, or the Duke and Duchess of Vanholt; the
other with the clowns Robin and Dick, the Horse
Courser, and the Carter. Again, the clowns occasionally parody the behavior of the hero: Faustus and
Mephistophilis steal from the Pope while Dick and
Robin steal from the Vintner.

During much of this action Faustus shows little
uneasiness. There is no suggestion of apprehension,
regret, or remorse until the end of the fourth act,
until, in fact, Faustus's "fatal time draws to a final
end." The events in Rome and Germany represent
the kind of activity and the manner in which Faustus
spent the twenty-four years of his contract. Our
dissatisfaction or discontent may be precisely the appropriate reaction, for we are watching Faustus as he
lives by his pact with Lucifer. The waste, the futility,
the loss of achievement by a man whose accomplishments might have been extraordinary is a central part
of his tragedy, and the middle of the play documents
this misuse of potential. Gradually Faustus is dimin-
ished in aspiration. His loss in stature is reflected also
by his loss in status. The clowns and comic episodes,
earlier kept separate from the Faustus story, by the
end of Act IV include Faustus himself, who becomes
involved in witless incidents with the Horse Courser
and the Carter. The scholar has himself finally become the clown.

Act V resumes the dramatic imagery and irony encountered at the opening. Faustus is found once more feasting, at "belly-cheer" with some Wittenberg students. At their request he invokes a vision of Helen of Troy that one guest calls ironically a "blessed sight," a sight for which Faustus should be "Happy and blest . . . evermore." Helen will reappear, but before she is recalled Faustus converses with a character simply called Old Man. He implores Faustus to repent, claiming that it is still not too late to gain salvation. He admits his exhortation may seem "harsh and all unpleasant"—words similar to Faustus's earlier description of divinity as "unpleasant, harsh, contemptible, and vile"—but Faustus is not beyond the power of mercy and forgiveness if he will seek it. The Old Man, like Good Counsel, his allegorical counterpart in the morality drama, knows that Faustus is not irremediably damned. Faustus will deserve absolute damnation not for his contract, not even for his past, but for his continued determination to perservere in the forbidden.

Once again Faustus expresses regret, but once again he despairs. "I do repent, and yet I do despair./ Hell strives with grace for conquest in my breast." Despair is the consequence of his inadequate faith, the suffering that comes from doubting that he can be saved. Unable to deny that part of his nature that first turned to black magic, Faustus cannot reconcile opposing desires at conflict within him. Mephistophilis reappears tempting Faustus with suicide and threatening him with physical pain. This, once more, persuades the scholar to reconfirm his vow to Lucifer, and he directs Mephistophilis to torment the Old Man. But the irony is again explicit, for if one has faith, Mephistophilis confesses he can do little harm:

His faith is great; I cannot touch his soul,
But what I may afflict his body with
I will attempt, which is but little worth.

Faustus's inability to believe in God's forgiveness is in itself an obstacle to his salvation. To fear damnation, to renounce magic, even to curse Mephistophilis and repent is insufficient. True repentence and true faith have positive effects; they are accompanied by confidence in the gift of grace. To doubt that he can be saved is to doubt that grace is freely given; to despair of his worth to heaven is to distrust the mercy of God. And without such trust and confidence salvation is impossible. "We must sin,/ And so consequently die . . . an everlasting death," Faustus has said. Lucifer, too, tells Faustus that "Christ cannot save thy soul, for he is just." These words repeat the arguments of Despair written by Marlowe's great contemporary Edmund Spenser.

Is not he just, that all this doth behold
From highest heaven, and beares an equall eye?
Shall he thy sins up in his knowledge fold,
And guiltie be of thine impietie?
Is not his law, Let every sinner die;
Die shall all flesh?

The Faerie Queene, I, ix, 47

If "sweet pleasure" had not conquered "deep despair," suicide, the temptation of Spenser's allegorical figure, would have long ago claimed Faustus its victim.

Scarce can I name salvation, faith, or heaven;
But fearful echoes thunder in mine ears:
"Faustus, thou art damned!" Then swords and knives,
Poison, guns, halters and envenomed steel
Are laid before me to dispatch myself;
And long ere this I should have done the deed,
Had not sweet pleasure conquered deep despair.

Marlowe chose to ignore, in his play, what Richard Hooker, the officially appointed apologist of the Anglican Church, calls man's "promise of God"; "I will not leave thee nor forsake thee." On this promise, Hooker builds his case for man's salvation.

> The simplicity of faith which is in Christ taketh the naked promise of God, his bare word, and on that it resteth. This simplicity the serpent labour-eth continually to pervert, corrupting the mind with many imaginations of repugnancy and con-trariety between the promise of God and those things which sense or experience or some other fore-conceived persuasion hath imprinted.[4]

With the threat of instant pain and damnation, what Hooker calls "imaginations of repugnancy and con-trariety," Lucifer brings Faustus to recant, to renew his vow, or with such parades as the Seven Deadly sins, indeed "laboureth continually to pervert" the mind.

To "glut" his appetite but also to distract his thoughts from his commitment to Lucifer, Faustus asks for Helen as his paramour. She reenters and the scholar glorifies her role in the siege of Troy.

> Was this the face that launched a thousand ships
> And burnt the topless towers of Ilium?
> Sweet Helen, make me immortal with a kiss.
> Her lips suck forth my soul. See where it flies
> Come, Helen, come, give me my soul again.
> Here will I dwell, for heaven is in these lips,
> And all is dross that is not Helena.

Power and beauty are her attributes as destruction and devastation are the effects most closely associated with her. The thousand ships that came to burn Troy's "topless towers" set sail to retrieve Helen, and the flames of that war foreshadow the hellfires that will

soon blaze for Faustus: "Instead of Troy shall Wittenberg be sacked"—it is about to lose its most famous
scholar.

In a parody of the communion service, Faustus
partakes not of the godhead but of the lips of a spirit
who draws forth his soul. In an ecstasy of passionate
exaggeration he announces that heaven is in her kiss.
Faustus imagines himself playing "hapless Semele" to
Helen's "flaming Jupiter," and like the Semele of Greek
myth, Faustus, too, will be consumed in a blazing
flame. Finally, Faustus compares his life to Arethusa,
the fountain that receives the dying light of the sun.
As they leave to consummate their love, the Old Man
announces that Faustus is to be forever damned. Having
rejected the grace of heaven Faustus cannot now be
saved and the Old Man goes to "fly unto my God."

From this point to the conclusion of the drama
there is no hope of Faustus's redemption. In an important study of the play, Sir Walter Greg pointed
out that, before Faustus makes love to Helen, the Old
Man tells Faustus that his "amiable soul" can still be
saved; after Faustus has left with her, however, the
Old Man suggests there is no possibility of forgiveness.
Faustus has refused "celestial happiness/ Pleasures un-
speakable, bliss without end." His fate may well be
affected by the special sin of demoniality.[5] Love of an
evil spirit, union with a demon, is the final action of
Faustus's magic that in the words of the Old Man "will
charm thy soul to hell/ And quite bereave thee of
salvation."

Although it is clear that Faustus is not to attain
the power and knowledge that he wishes, still, by his
daring he is a heroic figure courageously violating the
conventions of society and symbolically representing
the spirit of Renaissance optimism. Whatever is narrow

or ungenerous, whatever is confining or petty, he rejected in the beginning. Confidence and magnanimity
are an essential part of his nature—but not the whole
of that nature. His longing to experience the ultimate
in power and knowledge and his thirst to exceed the
limitations of mankind doom him to failure, to frustration and damnation. The insatiability characteristic of
Faustus's appetite leaves him gnawed by apprehension
and self-doubt, and these emotions inevitably give rise
to the most profound expression of Renaissance pes-
simism.

In his last meeting with his friends at Wittenberg,
Faustus takes his farewell in a prose passage expressing
the pain and sorrow of his situation as effectively as
any blank-verse writing.

> And what wonders I have done, all Germany can
> witness—yea, all the world—for which Faustus
> hath lost both Germany and the world, yea
> heaven itself, heaven the seat of God, the throne
> of the blessed, the kingdom of joy, and must re-
> main in hell for ever. Hell, ah hell for ever! Sweet
> friends, what shall become of Faustus, being in
> hell for ever?

The speech is carefully structured of brief phrases that
build to a climax. The parallelism of the language is
deliberate but not artificial; the triple repetition of "in
hell for ever," which ends the speech, gives the words a
terrible weight suggesting the resignation, the regret,
the fear of the speaker.

Awaiting the stroke of twelve, Faustus is granted
a vision of his future as the Bad Angel displays the
torments of men who were "gluttons and loved only
delicates." It is appropriate that he will suffer by way
of what gave him so much pleasure; his appetite is both
cause and means for him to "taste the smart of all."

After the vision of hell and the menacing promises of the Bad Angel, the clock strikes eleven and Faustus is alone.

Marlowe has with great subtlety prepared his audience for the soliloquy that follows; the spectator has been encouraged to empathize fully with the dying Faustus. The atmosphere established in the theater before his last words are spoken shares no small part in their effectiveness. The ability to engage the listener simultaneously in the thought of the speaker and the emotional excitement of his language is nowhere better displayed by Marlowe than in this closing speech, a soliloquy that has seldom been matched in English drama. Faustus's discussion, though abstract and spiritual, is expressed in simple and concrete images, while the intensity of his feeling is conveyed primarily through meter, rhythm, and phrasing. The soliloquy itself falls into three verse paragraphs each beginning with a desire that Faustus comes to realize cannot be fulfilled.

Now hast thou but one bare hour to live,
And then thou must be damned perpetually.
Stand still, you ever-moving spheres of heaven,
That time may cease and midnight never come,
Fair nature's eye, rise, rise again, and make
Perpetual day; or let this hour be but
A year, a month, a week, a natural day,
That Faustus may repent and save his soul.
O lente, lente currite noctis equi!
The stars move still; time runs; the clock will
    strike;
The devil will come, and Faustus must be damned.
O, I'll leap up to my God! Who pulls me down?

The urgency of the situation, with "but one bare hour to live," is suggested by the deliberate opposition of words involving motion: "Stand still" versus "ever-moving"; "cease" versus "come"; or "leap up" versus "pulls . . . down." And Marlowe uses other devices here—simple repetition, "Rise, rise again"; doubling the adverb in the quotation from Ovid, *"Lente, currite noctis equi"*; or contracting the scope of his references generally from the eternal and universal to the momentary and particular—to add to this sense of urgency. "Bare hour" is set off against "damned perpetually"; a plea for an extension of time is telescoped, "A year, a month, a week, a natural day." The striking clock that frames and divides the soliloquy points up the very futility of his words.

With the realization of his helplessness, with the acknowledgment of the irresistible movement of time, Faustus turns directly to God.

> See, see where Christ's blood streams in the firma-
> ment!
> One drop would save my soul, half a drop! Ah,
> my Christ!
> Rend not my heart for naming of my Christ!
> Yet will I call on him. O spare me, Lucifer!
> Where is it now? 'Tis gone. And see where God
> Stretcheth out his arm and bends his ireful brows.
> Mountains and hills, come, come, and fall on me,
> And hide me from the heavy wrath of God.

But attempting to hide from God's "ireful brows" is as impossible as seeking to move outside of time. If time's motion cannot be stopped, if God's harsh judgment cannot be evaded, Faustus then seeks some limit to his punishment.

> Let Faustus live in hell a thousand years,
> A hundred thousand, and at last be saved.

Again he realizes almost despite himself that his wish is futile: "The clock will strike"; "earth . . . will not harbor me"; "no end is limited to damnèd souls." Even the most imaginative escapes—to "leap up to my God," or to order stars to "draw up Faustus like a foggy mist," or to transform by metempsychosis "This soul . . . / Into some brutish beast"—are vain. Finally, he can no longer avoid acknowledging his fate: his soul "must live still to be plagued in hell." Faustus's all-consuming desire for knowledge meets its final rejection in the pledge to burn his books, and his soliloquy ends with a cry to Mephistophilis.

> My God, my God, look not so fierce on me!
> Adders and serpents, let me breathe a while!
> Ugly hell, gape not! Come not, Lucifer!
> I'll burn my books! Ah, Mephistophilis!

We learn of Faustus's terrible end in the next scene. Having heard shrieks and cries the night before, "twixt the hours of twelve and one," three scholars come to assure themselves that Faustus is safe and well. Instead, in horror, they find his limbs, "All torn asunder by the hand of death."

The Chorus, having opened the play, returns now to close it. Though its message is clearly moralistic, the reference to the permission required from heavenly powers for attaining knowledge emphasizes the subservience of man's position, the mercilessness of forces greater than man. This closing speech "exhorts the wise / Only to wonder" but not "to practise." Such advice and such wisdom are properly fit for the unheroic, for the timid and the shy. Divine law and the harshness with which it is enforced place, on human knowledge and aspiration, limitations that Faustus has dared to exceed; a man of his temperament naturally would reject such restrictions. The deity that Faustus describes behind this law is hardly Christian, and he is surely not quick to "cleanse" or to "forgive."

Faustus's God is without mercy or pity, a God harsher than he is in the Old Testament.

Faustus's conception of God may seem surprising to some, but it is even more surprising that the action of the play shows he is correct. Religion here is indeed a Christianity without Christ. Lucifer is quite right when he tells Faustus that "Christ cannot save thy soul, for he is just." Even when the hero in his final plea for salvation asks for mercy in the name of the sacrifice of Christ, his appeal is denied. The theology that Faustus rejected was quite accurate if it set subservience, servility, and absolute faith as requisites for redemption.

But what Faustus sought in place of Christian submissiveness—knowledge, self-fulfillment, pleasure—are also shown ultimately to be without value; absolute self-indulgence is not absolutely satisfying. Marlowe's romanticism is not simple here: he sees clearly that neither course open to Faustus is satisfactory. Although the poetry occasionally applauds the insatiability of Faustus's desires—

Have not I made blind Homer sing to me
Of Alexander's love and Oenon's death?
And hath not he, that built the walls of Thebes
With ravishing sound of his melodious harp,
Made music with my Mephistophilis?

—the play is nevertheless a profoundly pessimistic work. As a morality drama it fails to uphold the justice of its Christian framework; as a tragedy of extreme self-indulgence it proves how such a way of life is shallow and self-destructive. The glorified potential of man is matched but not overwhelmed by the realization of human limitation. The genius of Marlowe's poetry enabled him to celebrate while he despaired.

The first entry for "docter ffostose" in Henslowe's *Diary* is dated 30 September 1594; the play must have been popular, for it remained in the active repertory for the next three years.[6] In his inventory for the Admiral's Men in 1598, Henslowe included the "dragon in fostes," and Edward Alleyn, the leading actor with the company, noted "faustus Jerkin his clok." In addition, descriptions of the staging mention the appearance of frightening devils, or the use of thunder and firecrackers. A slightly later account describes Alleyn's appearance in "a surplis,/ With a crosse upon his breast"; presumably this was his costume at the opening of the play. A revival was evidently planned in 1602, for Henslowe arranged the payment to William Byrd and Samuel Rowley for "ther adicyones in docter fostes." *Doctor Faustus* was also acted by a company of English players at Graz, Austria, in 1608.

The work was still being staged during the reign of Charles II (1625–49), shortly before the Puritans closed the theaters in 1642. The very popularity of the work explains the special malice of the Puritans, who attacked those "prophanely playing the History of Faustus," horribly invoking the "visible apparition of the Devill on the stage of the Bel-savage Play-house . . . there being some distracted with that feareful sight."[7]

Another measure of the popularity of the play is the frequency of editions: at least nine printings had appeared between 1604 and 1631. Even after the Puritans closed the theaters, the work retained its hold on the reading public; eight new editions were published during the interregnum.

When the playhouses reopened in 1660, the story proved popular once more, for "Dr. Fostus" was acted at the Cock Pit in Drury Lane early in the 1660s, and Samuel Pepys took his wife to the Red Bull in May 1662, "where we saw 'Doctor Faustus,' but so wretchedly and poorly done that we were sick of it."[8] Perhaps it was this revival that prompted the 1663 edition of the play, printed "with New Additions as it is now Acted." A performance by the Duke's Company in 1675 even enjoyed the attendance of Nell Gwyn, the famous mistress of Charles II.

In pantomimes and puppet shows *Doctor Faustus* survived in the eighteenth century. In 1723 two rival pantomimes were playing in London—"Harlequin Doctor Faustus" at the Drury Lane and "The Necromancer: or, Harlequin's Doctor Faustus" at Lincoln's Inn Fields.[9]

Productions of *Doctor Faustus* in the nineteenth century were very largely translations of Goethe's drama. Only at the turn of the century did William Poel and the Elizabethan Stage Society mount Marlowe's play, first in 1896 and again in 1904. The play was staged at the Canterbury Festival in 1929, by the Old Vic in Liverpool in 1942, and in London in 1944. Next it appeared during the 1946–47 season at Stratford-on-Avon, first with Hugh Griffith, then with Paul Scofield playing Mephistophilis. In 1948 another Old Vic production was mounted in London with Cedric Hardwicke as Faustus. The Edinburgh Festival in 1961 saw a version directed by Michael Benthall. Many amateur and university productions have been staged in England, and the BBC arranged nine radio broadcasts since 1929 and a television production in 1947.

More recently, *Doctor Faustus* was produced by the Royal Shakespeare Company in London in 1968, with Eric Berry as Faustus. In 1965, the Oxford

Dramatic Society had staged a performance at Oxford, with Richard Burton and Elizabeth Taylor. This production was filmed in 1968.

The first American production of the work was in 1907 at Princeton. In 1968 the Royal Shakespeare Company production, with Eric Berry, was brought to Los Angeles.

The most notable American staging of *Doctor Faustus*, however, was sponsored by the Works Progress Administration in 1937, when Orson Welles played Faustus, and Jack Carter, Mephistophilis. On a stage "virtually stripped of scenery and decoration, relying upon an ingenious use of lights . . . ," the actors played on an apron built out over the orchestra pit,

> cheek by jowl with the audience. . . . The result is a *Doctor Faustus* that is physically and imaginatively alive, nimble, active—heady theatre stuff. . . . Orson Welles gives a robust performance that is mobile and commanding, and he speaks verse with a deliberation that clarifies the meaning and invigorates the sound of words. . . . Mr. Welles and [director John] Houseman have gone a long way to revolutionizing the staging of Elizabethan plays. [Brooks Atkinson, *New York Times*, 9 January 1937.]

Welles undertook the role again in 1950 in Paris, an unusual production in which Eartha Kitt played Helen, and for which Duke Ellington provided music.

Edward II

Edward II and Doctor Faustus are Marlowe's most mature works. This maturity can be found in the complexity and range of themes, in the subtlety and intelligence of their characterization, and, finally, in the control and refinement of their dramatic structure and poetry. The deliberate shaping of the plot and the unity of tone are further evidence of Marlowe's progress as an artist, of how far and how quickly he traveled. No longer is one troubled by the kind of episodic structure found in *Tamburlaine the Great*, with its flights of lyricism, or by the kind of inconsistent action found in *The Jew of Malta*, with its tone vacillating between melodrama and farce. By contrasting the earlier and the later works, one realizes with astonishment the rapidity of Marlowe's development as a dramatist in some half a dozen years.

Shakespeare's first history plays may well have influenced Marlowe, but he read many of the same chronicle sources with a very different eye. *Edward II*, his only English history play, bears Marlowe's distinctive stamp. Shakespeare's dramatizations of the chronicles all reflect his deep concern with the fate of

England, which provides a focal point for the actions and personalities of her rulers. Marlowe's treatment of the material—most of which was derived from the writings of the chroniclers Raphael Holinshed, John Stow, and Robert Fabyan—emphasized the interaction of personalities rather than politics revealing itself through character.

In *Edward II* Marlowe compressed and rearranged the tangled events of some thirty years into a structure that is neither strictly historical nor fundamentally political. He reshuffled the jumble of history to probe the psychology of his characters.

Edward II is built out of a series of peripeteia, or reversals. Following the plot is made more interesting if one remembers that every state may yield its opposite: happiness may give way to sorrow, success to failure, and defeat to victory. Out of such a chain of sudden changes in emotion and fortune is the play shaped. A few examples will make this clear. In the opening scene Gaveston, King Edward's favorite, is recalled to England from banishment by the newly crowned Edward, but the joyous king is soon forced by the nobles to exile him again. When Gaveston again returns to Edward in the second act, their reunion leads to death and civil war. In Act III the king defeats the nobles after Gaveston's murder, but he is himself defeated and murdered at the end of the play. Although the content of Marlowe's drama was dictated to a great extent by his choice of subject, his selection and arrangement of the events described in his sources were determined by the rhythmic substructure of these reversals. Each incident dovetails into the overall design of the drama. Despite the involved plot, the wealth of detail, and the highly individualized characters, Marlowe achieved a unity of tone and mood in *Edward*

II that he failed to accomplish in much of his earlier writing.

These reversals suggest the source of irony and the sense of frustration that prevail in the play. *The Jew of Malta* juxtaposes those who keep their word and those who break it; accordingly, the making of promises and vows is central to the meaning of that work. *Edward II* involves unsatisfied desires: the dialogue therefore is full of expressions of volition highlighting the constant opposition of one will to another or the antagonism between personal interest and public welfare. These battle lines are drawn, for example, with the very first appearance of Edward. The young king declares, "I'll have my will, and these two Mortimers,/ That cross me thus, shall know I am displeased." Again, a few lines later Edward insists, "I will have Gaveston." Twice in this scene he uses the same phrase when he refuses to heed anyone who would thwart his desires: to the threats of the nobles he announces, "I cannot brook these haughty menaces"; and to his brother's suggestion that he is overgenerous to Gaveston, Edward answers, "I cannot brook these words."

Edward is not the only one in the play to use such terms. His rivals, the barons led by the younger Mortimer and Warwick, also reveal their egos through their language. Speaking of Gaveston, Warwick asks the king, "Think you that we can brook this upstart pride?" and Mortimer threatens that he and the barons shall "either have our wills or lose our lives." For every time that Edward says, "We will have it so," or "how hardly can I brook," Warwick counters with "I will have that Gaveston," or Mortimer boasts, "I do what I will." All these major characters are men of uncontrolled pride and self-indulgence; they could never be expected to manage the government of a kingdom peaceably. Even Edward's favorites seem to take more pleasure in their own hedonism than in their regard for him. Gaveston plans to "Draw the pliant king which way I please"; he, too, complains of the nobles' insults: "I cannot brook these injuries." For Gaveston as well as for Spencer, his later replacement as the object of Edward's affection, having one's own way is everything.

Edward most fully reveals this total self-absorption in personal desires during the first of his forced partings from Gaveston: "And only this torments my wretched soul,/ That, whether I will or no, thou must depart." Edward makes it clear that their impending separation is not so painful to him as the fact that he is not a free agent. That Gaveston must leave "whether I will or no" is for Edward the real reason Gaveston's banishment is so agonizing.

The youthful king makes no attempt to restrain his emotions or to moderate his personal behavior. The ability to compromise, to reconcile the conflict between external responsibilities and inner drives, has never developed in him; self-satisfaction is all. There is something of the child in Edward, in his determination to have everything his way. And like the spoiled child, Edward is bad-tempered, stubborn, headstrong, and reckless. In Act I his attack on the Bishop of Coventry for his role in Gaveston's first exile is foolish and self-defeating, and his treatment of his wife, Isabella, cruel and impolitic.

A terrible honesty and directness govern this ruler whose only motivation is self-indulgence. A young prince, forthright and frivolous, can mature into a fine sovereign: high-spirited, warm, of a free and open nature. But these potentialities of youth can also soon become the liabilities of adulthood. Without tact, prudence, or sympathy, Edward's bluntness and egotism are not traits that improve with age. It proves false hope to think that "riper years would wean him from such toys."

These "toys," or distractions, are the extravagances encouraged by Gaveston, a consequence of the king's sexual attachment to him. Edward's homosexuality is not in itself of particular concern in determining his fitness to reign. To some, his nature still "promiseth as much as we can wish," and even to Mortimer, the "wanton humor" of the king's love is not of itself important. What is important, however, is influence over the king. And Edward, emotionally dependent on Gaveston, is totally controlled by him. From the time of their second reunion in Act II, Edward increasingly gives himself up to pleasure. His continual irresponsibility comes to have severe personal and political consequences, for the effects on the government grow progressively more serious: insurrection, rebellion, and civil war at home, and aggression by France, Ireland, Scotland, and Denmark abroad. To cope with the dangers that Lancaster and Mortimer relate, Edward would have earlier yielded them the necessary money and authority. But now accustomed to years of gratifying his own tastes exclusively, Edward has hardened. He can no longer be forced to rule his kingdom: he cannot even govern himself. The difficult, undisciplined, and uncorrected youth has grown into an obstinate man.

Marlowe emphasizes the important change that has been taking place in Edward's personality and the crucial effect it has on the country through the responses of the Earl of Kent, Edward's brother. Kent is perhaps the only major character in the play whose behavior is free from the taint of personal interest. He therefore functions for the audience as the indicator of a morally sound position in the conflict between Edward and his enemies. Kent aligns himself first with the king, later shifts to the support of the rebels, and, at the conclusion of the play, returns to argue the justness of Edward's cause. Although he twice defends Gaveston against the barons, Kent sensibly counsels Edward to use moderation, and in Act I he warns the king and Gaveston against attacking the Bishop of Coventry. His break with the king, near the end of Act II, occurs immediately after Edward refuses to answer the complaints of Lancaster and Mortimer; by this time Kent has come to realize that his brother's love for Gaveston "will be the ruin of the realm and you." With terrible scorn the king turns him away: "Whine thou with Mortimer." Kent joins the opposition, and in the struggle that follows Gaveston is executed.

When the nobles are finally defeated in the civil war that follows Gaveston's death, Kent helps Mortimer escape from the Tower, where Edward has imprisoned him. Together they join Queen Isabella and Prince Edward, who had left England earlier. Kent's opposition to the king is directed solely at forcing a reformation in his character: "Would all were well and Edward well reclaimed,/ For England's honor, peace, and quietness." He agrees to the necessity of renewing the conflict against the crown only after he has been convinced by Mortimer that Edward will otherwise never change: "But by the sword, my lord, it must be deserved;/ The king will ne'er forsake his flatterers."

Mortimer, the most forceful spokesman for the nobles, emerges as the leading antagonist to Edward. From the beginning of the play, he is fully aware of the need to separate the opposition to Edward's

flatterers from the quarrel with Edward's right to rule.
Mortimer argues with the nobles that to raise an army
against the king is rebellion and such an enterprise
could never win public support; to rally the people
against Gaveston and the men who mislead their
sovereign, however, would be easy. Should Edward's
flatterers not yield to the influence of the nobles, then,
Mortimer argues, the lords may

> with some color rise in arms;
> For howsoever we have borne it out
> 'Tis treason to be up against the king;
> So shall we have the people of our side,
> Which for his father's sake lean to the king,
> But cannot brook a night-grown mushrump.

When he speaks these words in Act I, Mortimer is
voicing an upright and honest opinion. But by the
fourth act, he, too, has changed. On this subject of
loyalty to the crown, his actions no longer support a
claim that Edward should continue to rule.

Near the end of Act IV when Mortimer, Kent,
Isabella, and Prince Edward land in England to mount
an offensive against the king, Mortimer rudely prevents the queen from concluding her apologia. He
realizes how impolitic it would be for Isabella publicly
to question Edward's right to continue ruling, and she
seems on the verge of making exactly this point.

> Misgoverned kings are cause of all this wrack;
> And, Edward, thou art one among them all
> Whose looseness hath betrayed thy land to spoil
> And made the channels overflow with blood.

Mortimer shifts the direction of this attack away from
Edward, stressing the legitimate claims of the queen
and prince, closing his peroration with the lines: "and

withal/ We may remove these flatterers from the king/ That havocs England's wealth and treasury."

According to Mortimer, he and the queen are not rebellious, but loyal; they seek not revolution, but reformation. Marlowe subtly implies, however, that their actions will prove contrary to their words. The abruptness with which Mortimer prevents the queen from continuing—"Nay, madam, if you be a warrior,/ You must not grow so passionate in speeches"—the quickness with which he alters her position, and, finally, the astuteness with which he fashions a defense indicate that he and Isabella are, in fact, in league. It is not surprising that some twenty lines later we learn from Kent that they "do kiss while they conspire."

Mortimer's potential for Machiavellian politics was made clear very early in the play. Arguing for the recall of Gaveston in Act I, Mortimer astutely realizes that the king's favorite is less dangerous to the barons in England where he can be watched, curbed, or eliminated, than if he is banished, ranging free and wealthy among enemies in Ireland. And Mortimer seems to have some schooling in Machiavellian ways of handling opposition.

> How easily might some base slave be suborned
> To greet his lordship with a poinard,
> And none so much as blame the murderer.

He knows when the truth has been "finely dissembled," and he is wise to the use of agents to remove his enemies and maintain his claim to innocence.

Capable and clever, Mortimer overpowers Edward, imprisons him, and rules England by acting as Lord Protector to Edward's young son. Though one is devious and the other forthright, Mortimer and

Edward nevertheless have much in common. Both are strong-willed, proud, determined, and fiery-tempered. Mortimer threatens to "thunder such a peal into his ears/ As never subject did unto his king." His insistence is equal to Edward's angry vow of vengeance for Gaveston's death: "I will have heads and lives for him/ As many as I have manors, castles, towns and towers." Both are thought promising as young men, and both, as they grow older, prove self-seeking. Edward insists that the king is absolute, free to indulge himself in luxury and riot, and Mortimer tries to hold the same total control over the realm that he had earlier denied the king.

> I seal, I cancel, I do what I will.
> Feared am I more than loved; let me be feared.
> And when I frown, make all the court look pale.

Although the strength and aggressiveness of Mortimer are contrasted with the weakness and self-indulgence of Edward, neither man can wield power beneficently. Although their personalities are fundamentally different, power corrupts them both; they are unable to resist the temptation of placing private gain over common good. Just as they are deficient in their public duties, their private lives hardly remain above reproach. Edward's illicit relationship with Gaveston is easily matched by Mortimer's adulterous affair with the queen; and she, like Gaveston, is allowed to share in the tyrannical control of the government.

In defeat, however, the emotional and philosophical responses of the two men fully express their diverse natures: Edward develops in compassion and sensitivity, while Mortimer always remains stoic. Suffering ennobles Edward, but experience merely hardens Mortimer.

When in Act III he is captured by Edward and his allies executed, Mortimer never despairs. His resolution remains firm even as he is taken to the Tower.

What, Mortimer, can ragged stony walls
Immure thy virtue that aspires to heaven?
No, Edward, England's scourge, it may not be;
Mortimer's hope surmounts his fortune far.

Finally, in the last scene of the play, when he is proved responsible for the murder of the king and sentenced to die, Mortimer accepts his fate with chilling resignation.

Base Fortune, now I see that in thy wheel
There is a point, to which when men aspire,
They tumble headlong down. That point I
    touched,
And, seeing there was no place to mount up
    higher,
Why should I grieve at my declining fall?
Farewell, fair queen; weep not for Mortimer,
That scorns the world, and, as a traveler,
Goes to discover countries yet unknown.

This farewell summarizes that combination of classical stoicism and medieval fatalism most popularly expressed in the *Mirror for Magistrates*, a compendium of tales in which Marlowe could have read the story of Mortimer's rise and fall. The *de casibus* tradition, stressing the fickleness of fortune and the inevitable destruction of those who ride her wheel past the top, finds that the human will is ineffective. Mortimer's philosophy permits him to acknowledge that man's wishes are in vain, that determination and stamina are ultimately ineffectual in the struggle against the capriciousness of an arbitrary fate. Although the words of his last speech may not be distraught, they are nevertheless pessimistic. As Irving Ribner has noted, Mortimer's corruption proves that even the strong man can be seduced by power into Machiavellian politics, and that the Machiavel, by his very ambition, is self-destroying.[1]

Edward, however, defeated and in the hands of Mortimer, forced to surrender his crown, finds little solace in classical philosophy, in such preaching as his friend Baldock's "all live to die, and rise to fall." Although Edward knows his case is not uncommon— "But what is he whom rule and empery/ Have not in life or death made miserable?"—he still hopes to find charity and pity.

> O, hadst thou ever been a king, thy heart,
> Piercèd deeply with a sense of my distress,
> Could not but take compassion of my state.

Capable of more tenderness and affection than Mortimer, Edward seeks love, understanding, and finally forgiveness from his captors. The torments he suffers after his capture serve to deepen the humanity of his disposition. The egotism and pride of the formerly inconsiderate king are gradually supplanted by warmth and humility. Edward now seeks to accept the evils others have committed as his own and to expiate the wrongs that others have suffered for him.

> O Gaveston, it is for thee that I am wronged;
> For me both thou and both the Spencers died,
> And for your sakes a thousand wrongs I'll take.
> The Spencer's ghosts, wherever they remain,
> Wish well to mine; then tush, for them I'll die.

The last scene of Act IV and Act V are extraordinarily powerful, not least because Edward at first receives from others the kindness his sufferings have earned. Even Leicester and Berkeley, to whom Morti-

mer has entrusted his prisoner, prove jailers unwilling
to distress the unhappy king. Their consideration
of him and the depth of his remorse suggest that
Edward has been brought to sufficient atonement, that
he now deserves reconciliation and forgiveness. As
confirmation, we learn that Kent has been discovered
by Mortimer in a plot to release the king. Although
Kent formerly had fought against his brother, he now
fights to free him. Since the young son of Edward and
Isabella is too weak to countermand the orders of
Mortimer, Kent is led off to execution. The cruelty of
Mortimer and Isabella is steadily revealed through the
former king's misery.

Bereft of his crown, shaved in puddle water, imprisoned in a castle sewer, and tormented by incessant
drumming, the captive Edward endures a degree of
pain that heightens his humanity. "Speak curstly to
him; and in any case/ Let no man comfort him," are
Mortimer's instructions to his henchmen. The very
brutality of this treatment educates Edward to a new
and profound appreciation of man's need for compassion and forgiveness. One important measure of his
ultimate superiority to Mortimer is his ability to grasp
this lesson. Mortimer's stoic resignation to an indifferent fate, his total lack of moral compunction, make
him less noble than the broken wretch who has discovered the importance of charity, dignity, and compassion.

Marlowe increases our sympathy for Edward when
the tortured king in his filthy rags remembers other,
happier times:

> Tell Isabel, the queen, I looked not thus,
> When for her sake I ran at tilt in France
> And there unhorsed the Duke of Cleremont.

Half-starved, half-mad, Edward impresses even Mortimer's henchmen. Incapable of pity, they at least admire their prisoner's stamina. But Edward is not allowed to remain even in their uncharitable care. At last the murderer, the most diabolical of Edward's tormentors, Lightborn, demands his victim. Neither to Mortimer nor to the audience does Lightborn describe the chosen method of execution, but it is clear that the range and refinement of his technique are extraordinary.

> 'Tis not the first time I have killed a man.
> I learned in Naples how to poison flowers,
> To strangle with a lawn thrust through the throat,
> To pierce the windpipe with a needle's point,
> Or whilst one is asleep, to take a quill
> And blow a little powder in his ears,
> Or open his mouth and pour quicksilver down.
> But yet I have a braver way than these.

The character Lightborn is entirely Marlowe's addition to the story. His function in the play and his name, an Anglicizing of Lucifer, suggest that he is a Vice figure, a devil out of the old morality plays who has come to administer torments to damned souls. The inhuman cruelty of his actions heightens our sympathy for Edward. "So now/ must I about this gear," he announces as he enters Edward's dungeon, "Ne'er was there any/ So finely handled as this king shall be."

The shocking scene of the king's murder is powerful not only because of the fiendishness of Lightborn's plan, but also because of his deliberate baiting of the prisoner. The murderer toys with his victim like a cat with a mouse. He pretends to have "comfort and joyful news"; he feigns sympathy with Edward's plight: "And what eyes can refrain from shedding tears/ To see a king in this most piteous state?" Lightborn plays at tenderness; Edward's tale of sorrow "breaks my heart," Lightborn says, and he assures the truly pathetic man that his "hands were never stained with innocent blood." Suspicious but exhausted, Edward sleeps briefly in the care of the devil, as, in Act IV, he had rested his head on the lap of the Abbot at Neath. This moment of false security heightens the power of the scene. Finally, Edward, trembling with terror, wakes to ask again why Lightborn has come. Bored with the game, annoyed with Edward's fear and restlessness, which make him less easy a prey, Lightborn reveals his errand directly: "To rid thee of thy life."

Like Faustus, Edward is agonized by the knowledge of his impending death. In his appeal to Lightborn, he seeks consolation from religion as well as charity from man.

> These looks of thine can harbor naught but death.
> I see my tragedy written in thy brows.
> Yet stay awhile: forbear thy bloody hand,
> And let me see the stroke before it comes,
> That even then when I shall lose my life,
> My mind may be more steadfast on my God.

The depth of his anguish, the degree of his agony, suggest the injustice of Edward's murder. But repentence, reconciliation, and forgiveness are meaningless terms in a world of Mortimers and Lightborns. In such a world Edward's execution is as devoid of meaning as Mortimer's, with its stoic vision of an arbitrary fate. There is, then, little difference between their deaths if compassion and forgiveness have no place in man's history.

Edward is not a clever Machiavel like Mortimer, and so he loses power; but Mortimer, the Machiavel, loses control of the kingdom, too. According to

Ribner, "To be incapable of exercising power like Edward is to be destroyed; to exercise it fully is to destroy one's self like Mortimer"; and even the man of absolute integrity like Kent dies guilt-ridden and defeated.[2] The impossibility of determining the right course of action— the inseparable confusion of means, and methods, and morals—is central to Marlowe's treatment of *Edward II*. Kent functions as a kind of moral weather vane, and it is important for the development of the theme to note that his rectitude is finally worth little to himself, his king, or his country.

The structure of the play should be seen as an outgrowth of this theme. The reversal of roles, the rise of Mortimer with the fall of Edward and then Mortimer's own fall, reflects perfectly the ambiguous crossing of the lines of innocence and culpability. This pattern of ascending and descending fortunes that intersect at midpoint in the action is the most sophisticated that Marlowe attempted, more complex than *Tamburlaine the Great* or *Doctor Faustus* and more intricate than *The Jew of Malta*. While shaping the mass of chronicle incident into dramatic form, Marlowe also handled with astonishing skill the problem of constructing a drama having more than one major character: two central figures, Edward and Mortimer, are balanced; two supporting figures, Gaveston and Isabella, are counterparts; and Kent remains to provide some guidance in their conflict.

The action, however, seems to evolve free from the rigidity of a prearranged schematic organization, retaining a sense of the irregular contradictions and reversals of life itself. This is due, in part, to the kind of character Marlowe portrayed. As in *Doctor Faustus*, Marlowe sought to delineate development, the gradually changing nature of the personalities of his characters. He realized that men are altered by experience, and the historical figures in this drama reflect his observation. It is an obvious psychological insight, perhaps, but nevertheless one almost unnoticed in the writing of his predecessors. Marlowe was diligent, for example, in sketching the stages through which the loving queen, rejected, becomes the adulterous wife, revenged, or the process through which Edward matures. Although every step of their transformation is not registered in the play, sufficient motivation and reaction are recorded for the audience to appreciate how emotional and psychological stress can affect temperament and attitude.

Indeed, Marlowe's achievement is remarkable in the theater of the period not only for its psychology but also for its poetry. The range of poetic tone here is unusually wide. Examples of the formal style of high rhetoric can be found in Edward's vow of vengeance against the nobles, in Act III, or in the herald's message from the barons that follows it. But the verse generally has a new suppleness, an ease that permits a closer approximation to the give-and-take of conversational speech.

What is most notable in this play is the absence of those solo passages rich in Marlovian lyricism. Marlowe persevered in his effort to render his poetry serviceable to the plot, character, and theme. His exuberant delight in language, his spirited reveling in words, was controlled and directed to more dramatic ends. Although some of that earlier excitement is lost, much more has been gained. Although there is little of the imagery and fire of *Tamburlaine the Great*, the verse in *Edward II* at its best is able to communicate emotional effects and psychological insight simultaneously. The pathetic Edward, reluctantly relinquishing his crown, explains his actions at the same time he expresses the intensity of his feelings.

> Take it. What, are you moved? Pity you me?
> Then send for unrelenting Mortimer
> And Isabel, whose eyes, being turned to steel,
> Will sooner sparkle fire than shed a tear.
> Yet stay, for rather than I will look on them,
> Here, here!

Realizing that language in the theater is most successful when it reflects the character grappling with his situation, Marlowe learned to write dramatic instead of lyric blank verse. If we judge his plays by the complexity and range of their subject, by the profundity and subtlety of their meaning, and, finally, by the control and refinement of their characterization, structure, and poetry, *Edward II* is Marlowe's finest work.

According to its 1594 title page, the first performance of *Edward II* was acted by the Earl of Pembroke's Men, probably during the Christmas season of 1593–94. It is not clear if Henslowe or any of the companies working with him ever acquired the play, although he does mention two works, "The Spencers" and "Mortimer," which may have had some relation to Marlowe's version of Edward's history. The 1622 quarto notes that the play was performed by "the late Queenes Majesties Servants at the Red Bull," perhaps when they appeared there in 1617.

While earlier productions seem rare, the play has proved popular in this century. At Oxford, the Elizabethan Stage Society, under the direction of William Poel, produced the work in 1903, with Granville Barker as King Edward. It was performed at Birkbeck College in 1920. The Phoenix Society acted the play in London in 1923, and college productions were organized at Cambridge in 1926 and Oxford in 1933. Bert-holt Brecht and Lion Feuchtwanger composed a loose adaptation of Marlowe's play for the Münchener Kammerspiele in April 1926. This version was most recently revived by the National Theatre in London in 1968.

Since World War II *Edward II* has been produced three times in London: by Joan Littlewood at Strat-ford East, in 1956; by Toby Robertson at the Lyric, Hammersmith, in 1959; and by the touring Prospect Theatre Company at the Mermaid Theatre, in 1969.

It was the 1969 staging, originally produced for the Edinburgh International Festival under Toby Robert-son's expert direction, that has most successfully demonstrated Marlowe's skills at dramaturgy. Per-formed on a raked, circular platform, with elaborate costumes and carefully modulated lighting, the play was praised for its power and poetry both in Edinburgh and in London. Atmospheric music, composed for the production by Carl Davis, was used to emphasize the emotions in a manner not unlike that in classic melo-drama.

Edward's homosexual love, in Robertson's inter-pretation, "is made totally explicit . . . as is his haughty hysteria and willfulness." And for his portrayal of the tragic king, Ian McKellan was acknowledged as the most promising young actor in the British theater. ". . . Mr. McKellan's acting, controlled while pas-sionate, induces pity and understanding for this weak-est of kings, even though he wisely never once plays for our sympathy" (Clive Barnes, in the *New York Times*, 4 September 1969). Benedict Nightingale noted in his *New Statesman* review (5 September 1969) that, from the early stages of the play, "when Edward fairly seethes with repressed energy," to the very end, when "the creature that Lightborn finally dispatches is a raddled, defeated, pathetic old queer, weakly grappling with his executioner," McKellan offered a performance that strongly established the character and then steadily revealed his disintegration. So moving was the climax, that Robert Eddison, who portrayed Lightborn, won the coveted *London Daily Evening Standard* Award for the best player in a supporting role.

The first professional New York performance was given as a matinee sponsored by the American National Theatre and Academy at the Theatre de Lys on 12 February 1958. Robert Kidd played the king in what one critic called a "turbulent pageant . . . robust and moving."

In interviews conducted by the *New York Times* (7 April 1974), prominent theater personalities were asked what plays they would like to see revived on the New York stage. Director John Houseman answered: "With the emergence of a viable American acting ensemble such as the City Center Acting Company and with the fading of sexual inhibitions of our contemporary stage, it has become possible to realize a production [*Edward II*] that I have been dreaming of for more than a dozen years." Houseman's City Center Acting Company will include *Edward II* in their 1974–75 repertory.

Dido, Queen of Carthage

Dido, Queen of Carthage, probably his earliest play, is the only play Marlowe wrote for a children's company. In writing dramas for performance by a company of boy choristers, ranging in age from eight to thirteen years, a playwright naturally attempted to exploit their special skills and abilities. Generally this meant incorporating songs, shaping the text for ensemble playing, and anticipating clarity of enunciation, poise, and grace in the handling of dialogue.

The small, candlelit, indoor or "private" houses in which the boys appeared, such as the Blackfriars theater, imitated the setting of a court performance before Queen Elizabeth, and the coterie audience in attendance accordingly sought a much more costly and aristocratic entertainment than would have been found by the spectators at any of the larger public playhouses. Indeed, the private houses charged up to four times the price of admission of the public theaters, permitting such spectators to consider themselves wealthy and extravagant as well as sophisticated, educated, and well informed.

Stage production in the private houses probably used fixed, multiple sets in contrast to the bare public stages. The playing area for *Dido*, for example, could be divided into three locations by "mansions," or canvas-covered frames, to indicate perhaps on the left, the woods and a cave near Carthage, in the center rear, Mount Olympus, and, on the right, the walls of the city. The action of Marlowe's play lends itself to such an arrangement, and this tripartite division is in keeping with descriptions of staging both at court and at the Blackfriars.

Marlowe relied on Vergil's account of the defeat of Troy and the sojourn of Aeneas at Carthage, in Books I, II, and IV of the *Aeneid*, for the essential facts and details of *Dido, Queen of Carthage*. By adding and altering incidents and characters, however, he shaped this material to contrast the divine and human characters, to compare their situations, and to express his point of view.

The opening scene of the drama provides a good example of Marlowe's technique. Jupiter is dandling his beautiful catamite, Ganymede, on his lap, defying Juno for love of the boy he has brought to Olympus. Such a scene at the start of the play establishes the audience's attitude toward the gods and provides a contrast to the story of Dido and Aeneas. This brief sketch of the gods in a forbidden love prefaces the tale of mortals in a love forbidden by the gods. Aeneas will later be allowed no choice but to reject Dido and follow the path ordered by the gods, and yet the king of the gods is himself first revealed as freely indulging his sexual appetite.

Marlowe provided further incidents that join the separate strands of the plot and thereby serve to con-

trast the divine and human characters. Just as Ganymede appears on Jupiter's lap in this scene, Cupid will
appear later, in Act III, on the lap of Dido and then on
the lap of Dido's nurse. (In fact, the roles of Cupid
and Ganymede may well have been played by the same
actor.) The uncontrollable emotions that Cupid can
bring about are seen to affect the gods as well as man;
but of the two, men behave in nobler fashion. The
material that Marlowe added to the *Aeneid* serves to
belittle the Olympian rather than the human characters.

After Venus has appealed to Jupiter for the safety of
her son, Aeneas, on his journey from Troy to Italy,
and after Jupiter has prophesied the future founding
of Rome, the play turns to Vergil's story and follows
closely the Latin narrative: Aeneas, shipwrecked on
the shore of Carthage, is prompted by his mother to
join with his men and find Dido, who can provide them
with the means of reaching Italy. Aeneas's brief account to Venus of his fortunes and his comparison of
Carthage and his native Troy prepare the audience for
the lengthy retelling of the last battle of Troy, an
account that Dido commissions from him almost immediately after they have met. Before Aeneas begins
his narrative, however, the queen offers her guest her
dead husband's robes and seats him in her place. In
fact, her welcome and encouragement—"Thy future
may be greater than thy birth"—exceed the bounds of
hospitality and suggest her immediate and strong attraction to the Trojan even before Cupid has intervened.

Act II is largely composed of Aeneas's narrative. The
description of the fall of Troy is a set piece of considerable poetic and dramatic dimension and in a very
different mode from Jupiter's prediction in Act I of

the founding of Rome. Jupiter's speech is formal in word and phrasing, conveying the dignity of the king of the gods at his most regal:

> Three winters shall he with the Rutiles war
> And in the end subdue them with his sword;
> And full three summers likewise shall he waste
> On managing those fierce barbarian minds.

But Aeneas's narrative, a version of the messenger speech of classical tragedy, attempts to convey the impression of immediacy by vividness of language and detail. In addition, Marlowe was proving his skill as a verse translator by rendering into English a passage that all educated members of his audience were sure to know. He demonstrated his virtuosity by remaining close enough to the original to remind his listener of Vergil's poetry, and by finding language that conveys in the fullest measure the intensity of the actions described. Marlowe retained the iambic pentameter line as a standard so that variations in meter could be used for additional expressive power.

By a careful arrangement of active verbs, Marlowe has Aeneas describe the entrance into Troy of the Grecian army and the joining of these soldiers with their compatriots who had been hidden in the wooden horse:

> By this, the camp was come unto the walls,
> And through the breach did march into the
>   streets,
> Where, meeting with the rest, "Kill, kill," they
>   cried.
> Frighted with this confused noise, I rose,
> And looking from a turret, might behold
> Young infants swimming in their parents' blood,
> Headless carcasses piled up in heaps,
> Virgins half-dead, dragged by their golden hair

And with main force flung on a ring of pikes,
Old men with swords thrust through their agèd
    sides,
Kneeling for mercy to a Greekish lad,
Who with steel pole-axes dashed out their brains.

Present participles link the stages of the narration—
"meeting," "looking," "swimming," "kneeling"—and
these are interwoven with a series of past participles
followed by prepositions: "Frighted with," "piled up,"
"dragged by," "flung on," "thrust through." To convey the frenzied activity, the verbs occur with increasing frequency.

Aeneas then recounts how he set out to oppose the
enemy. His lines continue to emphasize the action by
placing the verb before the subject: "buckled I mine
armor," "flung I forth."

Rhetorical devices, too, are carefully used by Marlowe. In his hands they are not just a decorative
means of embroidering the text, but more a technique
for heightened emotional expression. In Aeneas's account, Priam's plea to Achilles for mercy is a rigidly
balanced yet moving catalog of lost titles:

Father of fifty sons, but they are slain;
Lord of my fortune, but my fortune's turned;
King of this city, but my Troy is fired;
And am now neither father, lord, nor king.

Marlowe's powers of visual imagination and language
combine to produce phrases impressive for the forcefulness of their images. Aeneas recalls Hecuba's violent
separation from Priam: "At last the soldiers pulled her
by the heels/ And swung her howling in the empty
air"; or he remembers his final sight of the prophetess
Cassandra, "sprawling in the streets,/ Whom Ajax
ravished in Diana's fane"; and he describes his last

view of Pyrrhus: "leaning on his sword, he stood stone still,/ Viewing the fire wherewith rich Ilion burned."

The real importance of these lines for Elizabethan drama lies in the display of the versatility of the medium; in the hands of a playwright-poet, blank verse is capable of expressing the widest range of feelings with the greatest dramatic impact. The ease of Marlowe's control over poetic effects, the assurance of his use of stress, caesura, end-stopped and run-on lines for theatrical forcefulness is astonishing. Aeneas relates how Priam greeted the traitor Sinon: "Kissed him, embraced him, and unloosed his bands." The counterpoint of four speech stresses played against the standard iambic pentameter rhythm gives tension and emotion to the line. The line immediately following, imitating classical precedent, is a tetrameter and its loss of a foot supports the anacoluthon, a rhetorical device that allows emotion to interrupt the thought of the speaker: "And then—O Dido, pardon me!" The meaning, the action, and the emotional value are all conveyed by the words and supported by the metrical pattern that underlies their arrangement.

As Aeneas and Dido leave the stage, Venus, seeking further assurance that Aeneas will be helped, enters to arrange for the exchange of her son, Cupid, the god of love, with Ascanius, Aeneas's son. Both are the same age, and Cupid, disguised as Ascanius, is to cause the Carthaginian queen to dote on the Trojan leader.

This scene offers a change of mood. Venus sings a lullaby to Ascanius so the sleeping boy can be abducted. The lines broaden the range of the poetry, for the tone here is no longer narrative or formal but pastoral:

> Now is he fast asleep, and in this grove
> Amongst green brakes I'll lay Ascanius
> And strew him with sweet smelling violets,
> Blushing roses, purple hyacinth.

Cupid's success is then dramatized in the first scene of the third act. The god of love first reminds the audience of his purpose, charms his way near Dido, sings, hangs about her neck, and, finally, wounds her with his arrow. The torment of Dido, torn between her almost irresistible longing for Aeneas and the need to be civil to her present suitor, Iarbus, makes her both amusing and sympathetic. Her divided mind, her self-contradiction, is the result of her new passion, or, at least, is a measure of its strength. And her emotions are expressed in lines of rich and exaggerated imagery:

> I'll make me bracelets of his golden hair;
> His glistering eyes shall be my looking-glass,
> His lips an altar, where I'll offer up
> As many kisses as the sea hath sands.

Her response to Aeneas is even more extravagant when he appears.

> I'll give thee tackling made of rivelled gold,
> Wound on the barks of odoriferous trees,
> Oars of massy ivory, full of holes
> Through which the water shall delight to play,
> Thy anchors shall be hewed from crystal rocks
> Which if thou lose, shall shine above the waves;

Dido's struggle to suppress her feelings, her discretion and pride, her desire to be richly valued, to be wooed and won, are all sensitively handled in the lines that follow. Her appeal lies in her combination of power and delicacy, strength and finesse, authority and femininity. By position and responsibility she commands, but in her wisdom, she knows that not all things can be ruled—indeed, modesty prevents some things from even being named: "The thing that I will die before I ask,/ And yet desire to have before I die."

Dido's rejection of her suitor, Iarbus, provides Marlowe with still another opportunity to compare men and gods. Although Anna, Dido's sister, is secretly in love with Iarbus, she never declares her feelings openly until Dido has absolutely announced her determination to refuse him. This near rivalry is immediately contrasted in the following scene with the actions of another pair of women, two who "banquet as sisters with the gods," Venus and Juno. Envious of Venus, angered that she had not been chosen to receive the golden apple, Juno has set herself against Aeneas and his mother. Juno is scarcely so considerate or forgiving a woman as Anna, and she reviews once more all her reasons for hating and distrusting Venus. When the two goddesses meet in this scene, they agree, at least outwardly, to join forces to promote the love of Dido and Aeneas, but it is clear that theirs is an uneasy peace.

The love confession between Dido and Aeneas, which closes the third act, contains writing of a very high order. Marlowe's interest in character development and psychological behavior and his use of dramatic irony heighten the scene. The sincerity of Aeneas's vow contrasts ironically with our knowledge that, in fact, he will abandon Dido despite his oath.

> With this my hand I give to you my heart
> And vow by all the gods of hospitality,
> By heaven and earth, and my fair brother's bow,
> By Paphos, Capys, and the purple sea
> From whence my radiant mother did descend,
> And by this sword that saved me from the Greeks,
> Never to leave these new-upreared walls.

To emphasize his deliberate juxtaposition of divine and earthly lovers, Marlowe carefully has Dido echo the words of Jupiter when he tempted Ganymede. At the opening of the play, Jupiter had offered gifts:

> Hold here, my little love, these linked gems,
> My Juno wore upon her marriage day,
> Put thou about thy neck, my own sweetheart
> And trick thy arms and shoulders with my theft.

And now Dido offers gifts to Aeneas:

> Hold. Take these jewels at thy lover's hand,
> These golden bracelets, and this wedding ring
> Wherewith my husband wooed me yet a maid,
> And be thou king of Libya by my gift.

With Act IV the countermovement begins. First, Iarbus voices his jealousy of Aeneas. In the next scene Anna offers the frustrated Iarbus her love, only to find herself rejected as he was rejected by Dido and as Dido will be by Aeneas. That all three will ultimately choose the same death is indeed appropriate.

In the third scene Aeneas abruptly announces that Hermes, the messenger of the gods, has ordered his departure from Carthage, and, though reluctant to leave—"I fain would go, yet beauty calls me back"— he accepts the god's command. His first attempt to sail away is halted by Dido, who describes her pleasures with him in lines that are among the best Marlowe ever wrote:

> Heavens, envious of our joys, is waxen pale,
> And when we whisper, then the stars fall down
> To be partakers of our honey talk.

He is won over and agrees to remain in Carthage with her.

To insure that Aeneas will not try again to sail away,

Dido orders her elderly nurse to take the youth she believes to be Ascanius into the country. In the last scene of Act IV, the nurse carries Cupid in her arms as he teases her by arousing desires seemingly inappropriate for a woman of her years. Like Jupiter with Ganymede and Dido with Cupid, the nurse, too, talks of love with a boy in her arms. The foolishness and frustration of her longing are a comment on both the king of the gods and the queen of Carthage. Though she may seem the most ridiculous of the three, the nurse, in her rationalizing, summons up a powerful argument in her defense: "If there be any heaven in earth, 'tis love."

The last act begins with Hermes returning the abducted Ascanius to Aeneas and ordering him once more to leave Carthage. Iarbus, hoping to remove his competition, quickly agrees to supply Aeneas's ships with the equipment that Dido had withdrawn. Dido notices the activity on the shore and learns from Aeneas of Jupiter's repeated command. Dido makes her appeals first using rhetorical devices such as her pun on the meaning of "fare well" and the chiasmus, or balancing of phrases, in the last sentence of her reproach:

> Farewell? Is this the mends for Dido's love?
> Do Trojans use to quit their lovers thus?
> Farewell may Dido, so Aeneas stay;
> I die if my Aeneas say farewell.

Next, she tries conceits of a more Petrarchan kind:

> Why look'st thou toward the sea? The time hath been
> When Dido's beauty chained thine eyes to her.
> Am I less fair than when thou sawest me first?
> O, then, Aeneas, 'tis for grief of thee.
> Say thou wilt stay in Carthage with thy queen,
> And Dido's beauty will return again.

Finally, she accuses the gods themselves of injustice, of meddling in matters of profound concern to her: "Wherein have I offended Jupiter/ That he should take Aeneas from mine arms?" As we have seen already, the gods are indeed irresponsible in love, Jupiter with Ganymede, or, as Dido reminds us, Venus with Mars. Aeneas is their pawn and Dido is unfortunately their victim. The Trojan leader is the son of a goddess, but the queen of Carthage is a mortal and of no concern to the power brokers on Olympus. For them, she has been simply a means to attain their own ends. Their indifference to her fate is an aspect of their basic egocentricity and cruelty.

Dido now curses the man she cannot help but love. Revengeful, she wishes him ill fortune; but, she confesses, were Aeneas and his colleague, Achates, to lie dead on the shore, "I'll give ye burial/ And weep upon your lifeless carcasses,/ Though thou nor he will pity me a whit." As T. S. Eliot has noted, Dido's parting words sound almost Shakespearean:

> Leap in mine arms. Mine arms are open wide.
> If not, turn from me, and I'll from thee,
> For though thou hast the heart to say farewell,
> I have not power to stay thee.

Delirious, Dido imagines she sees Aeneas returning to her and fantasizes their reunion. She determines to burn "all that this stranger left." She curses the country that Aeneas will build, calls for incessant warfare between Carthage and Italy, and throws herself into the flames. In grief, Iarbus follows her, and Anna, in despair, destroys herself in the same fire.

At whatever stage of his career the play was written, Marlowe's accomplishment in *Dido, Queen of Carthage* is considerable. A part of this achievement is innovation in the genre itself. The pattern for children's company plays had largely been cut by John Lyly. Lyly's works dramatize variations on a central topic or portray the many examples of a common issue. In a highly refined manner, with delicacy and charm, his writing for the children's companies usually places emphasis on language and unifying conceit rather than on character and human relationships.

Marlowe borrowed from the storehouse of tricks in Lyly's arsenal, adopting those aspects of staging, music, parody, and multifaceted treatment of theme that Lyly had made characteristic of children's company plays. But where Lyly's artificial and rhetorical prose, with its balanced debates and linguistic elegance, deliberately reduces the intensity of any emotion, Marlowe's blank verse heightens it. Where Lyly studiously avoided thematic development and psychological portrayal, Marlowe carefully altered his sources to permit the dramatization of his theme and the analysis of his characters.

Marlowe's lavish rendering of Vergil's story into English blank verse does not share Lyly's linguistic or intellectual ordering. But then, the delicacy, the refinement characteristic of Lyly were not qualities of primary concern to Marlowe. The thematic development of his material, the additions to Vergil of the Jupiter-Ganymede, Iarbus-Anna, nurse-Cupid episodes may all provide variations on a theme of a Lylian sort, but they lead to an attitude and a conclusion that Lyly would have avoided. The cruelty of the gods and the suffering and sacrifice of an unrequited lover are not appropriate substance for the fragile artifice of a drama by Lyly. With Marlowe the passions, and the meaning, and the language are of a more robust composition. He thus extended the range of the plays written for children's companies, rejecting some of the restrictions that Lyly had imposed on these dramas.

In addition, Marlowe may have opened the way for children's plays in verse, for Lyly's only poetic drama dates from the early 1590s, in all probability well after Marlowe's play was written. The two men, after all, may have been rivals; they probably had been classmates at the King's School in Canterbury, and their association may have been renewed later by their mutual friendship with Thomas Nashe. It is Nashe who called Lyly "one of the best wits in England," and it is Nashe who claims coauthorship with Marlowe on the title page of *Dido, Queen of Carthage*. Actually, the extent of Nashe's responsibility for the text of the play is unclear. Marlowe's hand predominates, and Nashe, in fact, may have done little more than see the manuscript through the press; the play is thought to have been written exclusively by Marlowe.

Although *Dido, Queen of Carthage* was written for a children's company, much of its material is characteristic of what Marlowe later wrote for the adult players. The scenes of Dido and of her nurse with Cupid show a character in a state of indecision, and such unresolved mental conflict is similar to what Tamburlaine undergoes in weighing the opposing claims of warfare and love. The irresistible passion that Dido feels is also the subject of *Doctor Faustus*, as well as *Edward II*, and the personalities of all three of these title characters are strongly shaped by their experiences and their suffering. Finally, the attitude toward the gods in this play is close to that Marlowe expressed in his tragedies. Jupiter's amorality and essential indifference to man here parallels views found in the later works.

Its dialogue is less often dramatic, its poetry is less

often responsive to the limitations of stage performance than the plays for adult companies, but *Dido,
Queen of Carthage* remains an impressive achievement
for a dramatic poet of any age, at any stage of his
career.

Except for the claim on the title page of the 1594
printing, that *Dido, Queen of Carthage* was acted by
the Children of Her Majesty's Chapel, there are no
records indicating a performance of what we can be
sure was Marlowe's play until the twentieth century.
In 1964, as part of the four-hundredth anniversary
of Marlowe's birth, the play was performed by school-
boys from Southampton.

NOTES

CHRONOLOGY

1. Quoted in John Bakeless, *The Tragicall History of Christopher Marlowe*, Vol. I (Cambridge, Mass., 1942), p. 77.
2. Quoted in J. Leslie Hotson, *The Death of Christopher Marlowe* (New York, 1967), pp. 31–33.

MARLOWE AND ELIZABETHAN THEATER

1. Alfred Harbage, *Shakespeare's Audience* (New York, 1941), pp. 36, 41.
2. Bernard Beckerman, *Shakespeare at the Globe, 1599–1609* (New York, 1962), pp. 9ff.
3. George Burke Johnston, ed., *Poems of Ben Jonson* (Cambridge, Mass., 1968), Epigrammes LXXXIX, p. 41.

TAMBURLAINE THE GREAT, PART II

1. Ethel Seaton, "Marlowe's Map," *Essays and Studies* 10 (1924):13–35. See also: Seaton, "Fresh Sources for Marlowe," *Review of English Studies* 5 (1929): 385–401.

2. Paul Kocher, *Christopher Marlowe: A Study of His Thought, Learning, and Character* (North Carolina, 1946), pp. 84ff.
3. Quoted in E. K. Chambers, *The Elizabethan Stage*, Vol. II (Oxford, 1923), p. 135.
4. R. A. Foakes and R. T. Rickert, eds., *Henslowe's Diary* (Cambridge, 1961), pp. 23ff.

THE JEW OF MALTA

1. For two contrasting interpretations see: T. S. Eliot, *Selected Essays* (New York, 1950); and F. P. Wilson, *Marlowe and the Early Shakespeare* (Oxford, 1953).
2. For a discussion on this point, see: Alfred Harbage, "Innocent Barabas," *Tulane Drama Review* 4 (Summer 1964):47–58.
3. R. A. Foakes and R. T. Rickert, eds., *Henslowe's Diary* (Cambridge, 1961), pp. 16ff, 170.

THE MASSACRE AT PARIS

1. See H. J. Oliver, ed., *The Massacre at Paris* (Cambridge, Mass., 1968), p. lix.
2. R. A. Foakes and R. T. Rickert, eds., *Henslowe's Diary* (Cambridge, 1961), p. 20.
3. Ibid., pp. 22ff.
4. Ibid., pp. 82, 76.
5. Ibid., p. 183.
6. Ibid., p. 187.

DOCTOR FAUSTUS

1. The most detailed studies of the text of the play will be found in: W. W. Greg, *Doctor Faustus, 1604–16* (London, 1950); and Greg, *Doctor Faustus: A Conjectural Reconstruction* (London, 1950).
2. C. L. Barber, " 'The form of Faustus' fortunes good

or bad,'" *Tulane Drama Review* 4 (Summer 1964): 92–119.

3. See Cleanth Brooks and Robert B. Heilman, *Understanding Drama* (New York, 1948), pp. 532ff.

4. Richard Hooker, *A Learned and Comfortable Sermon of the Certainty and Perpetuity of Faith in the Elect of the Laws of Ecclesiastical Polity*, Vol. I (New York, 1963), pp. 8–9.

5. W. W. Greg, "The Damnation of Faustus," *Modern Language Review* 41 (1946):97–107.

6. R. A. Foakes and R. T. Rickert, eds., *Henslowe's Diary* (Cambridge, 1961), p. 24.

7. E. K. Chambers, *The Elizabethan Stage*, Vol. III (Oxford, 1923), pp. 423–24.

8. William van Lennep, Emmett L. Avery, et. al., *The London Stage*, Part I (Carbondale, Ill., 1960–65), p. 51.

9. *The London Stage*, Part II, p. cxviii.

Edward II

1. Irving Ribner, "Marlowe's 'Tragicke Glasse,' " in *Essays on Shakespeare and Elizabethan Drama* (Columbia, 1962), pp. 108ff.

2. Ibid., p. 108.

BIBLIOGRAPHY

1. EDITIONS OF MARLOWE'S WORKS

Case, R. H., gen. ed. *The Works and Life of Christopher Marlowe.* 6 vols. London, 1930–33.
  1. *Life* and *Dido, Queen of Carthage*, ed. C. F. Tucker Brooke.
  2. *Tamburlaine the Great, I and II*, ed. U. M. Ellis-Fermor.
  3. *The Jew of Malta* and *The Massacre at Paris*, ed. H. S. Bennett.
  4. *Poems*, ed. L. C. Martin.
  5. *Doctor Faustus*, ed. F. S. Boas.
  6. *Edward II*, ed. H. B. Charlton and A. R. Waller, revised by F. N. Lees, 1955.
Greg, W. W., ed. *Doctor Faustus, 1604–16.* London, 1950.
———. *Doctor Faustus: A Conjectural Reconstruction.* London, 1950.
Jump, J. D., ed. *Doctor Faustus.* Cambridge, Mass., 1962.
———. *Tamburlaine the Great, Parts I and II.* Lincoln, Nebr., 1967.
Merchant, W. Moelwyn, ed. *Edward the Second.* London, 1967.
Oliver, H. J., ed. *Dido, Queen of Carthage* and *The Massacre at Paris.* Cambridge, Mass., 1968.

Ribner, Irving, ed. *The Complete Plays of Christopher Marlowe*. New York, 1963.

Van Fossen, Richard, ed. *The Jew of Malta*. Lincoln, Nebr., 1964.

2. WORKS ABOUT MARLOWE

Allen, Don Cameron. "Marlowe's *Dido* and the Tradition." In *Essays on Shakespeare and Elizabethan Drama*. Ed. Richard Hosley. Columbia, Mo. 1962.

Bakeless, John. *The Tragicall History of Christopher Marlowe*. 2 vols. Cambridge, Mass., 1942.

Babb, Howard S. "Policy in Marlowe's *The Jew of Malta*." *Journal of English Literary History* 24 (1957):85–94.

Barber, C. L. " 'The form of Faustus' fortunes good or bad.' " *Tulane Drama Review* 4 (1964):92–119.

Battenhouse, Roy. *Marlowe's Tamburlaine: A Study in Renaissance Philosophy*. Nashville, Tenn., 1941.

Bevington, David. *From Mankind to Marlowe*. Cambridge, Mass., 1962.

———. *Tudor Drama and Politics*. Cambridge, Mass., 1968.

Bradbrook, Muriel. "Marlowe's *Doctor Faustus* and the Eldritch Tradition." In *Essays on Shakespeare and Elizabethan Drama*. Ed. Richard Hosley, Columbia, Mo., 1962.

———. *Themes and Conventions of Elizabethan Tragedy*. Cambridge, England, 1935.

Brooke, Nicholas. "Marlowe the Dramatist." In *Elizabethan Theatre*. Ed. John Russell Brown and Bernard Harris. London, 1966.

Brooks, Cleanth, and Robert Heilman. *Understanding Drama*. New York, 1945.

Brooks, Harold. "Marlowe and Early Shakespeare." In *Christopher Marlowe*. Ed. Brian Morris. London, 1968.

Chambers, E. K. *The Elizabethan Stage*. 4 vols. Oxford, 1923.

Cole, Douglas. *Suffering and Evil in the Plays of Christopher Marlowe*. Princeton, N.J., 1962.

Duthie, G. I. "The Dramatic Structure of Marlowe's *Tamburlaine the Great, Parts I and II.*" *English Studies*. Ed. F. P. Wilson. 1 (1948):101–26.

Eccles, Mark. *Christopher Marlowe in London*. Cambridge, Mass., 1934.

Eliot, T. S. "Christopher Marlowe." In *Selected Essays*. New York, 1950.

Foakes, R. A. "The Profession of Playwright." In *Early Shakespeare*. Ed. John Russell Brown and Bernard Harris. New York, 1961.

Foakes, R. A., and R. T. Rickert. *Henslowe's Diary*. Cambridge, England, 1961.

Gardner, Helen. "The Second Part of *Tamburlaine the Great*. *English Studies*. Ed. F. P. Wilson. 37 (1942): 18–24.

Gibbons, Brian. "Unstable Proteus: Marlowe's *The Tragedy of Dido, Queen of Carthage*." In *Christopher Marlowe*. Ed. Brian Morris. London, 1968.

Greg, W. W. "The Damnation of Faustus." *Modern Language Review* 41 (1946):97–107.

Harbage, Alfred. "Innocent Barabas." *Tulane Drama Review* 4 (1964):47–58.

———. *Shakespeare and the Rival Tradition*. New York, 1952.

———. *Shakespeare's Audience*. New York, 1941.

Harrison, G. B. *Elizabethan Plays and Players*. Ann Arbor, Mich., 1956.

Hooker, Richard. *Sermon on the Certainty and Perpetuity of Faith in the Elect*. New York, 1907.

Hotson, J. Leslie. *The Death of Christopher Marlowe*. New York, 1967.

Hunter, G. K. "Five-Act Structure in *Doctor Faustus*." *Tulane Drama Review* 4 (1964):77–91.

———. *Lyly and Peele*. London, 1968.

———. *John Lyly: The Humanist as Courtier*. London, 1962.

Johnston, George Burke, ed. *Poems of Ben Jonson*. Cambridge, Mass., 1968.

Izard, Thomas. "The Principal Source of Marlowe's *Tamburlaine*." *Modern Language Notes* 58 (1943): 411–17.

Kocher, Paul H. *Christopher Marlowe: A Study of His Thought, Learning, and Character.* Chapel Hill, N.C., 1946.

Leech, Clifford. "The Structure of *Tamburlaine*." *Tulane Drama Review* 4 (1946): 32–46.

Levin, Harry. *The Overreacher: A Study of Christopher Marlowe.* Cambridge, Mass. 1952.

The London Stage 1660–1800. Ed. William van Lennep, Emmett L. Avery, et. al., Carbondale, Ill., 1960–65.

Mahood, M. M. *Poetry and Humanism.* London, 1950.

Mizener, Arthur. "The Tragedy of Marlowe's *Doctor Faustus*." *College English* 5 (1943): 70–75.

Morris, Harry. "Marlowe's Poetry." *Tulane Drama Review* 4 (1964): 134–54.

Mulryne, J. R., and Stephen Fender. "Marlowe and the 'Comic Distance.'" In *Christopher Marlowe.* Ed. Brian Morris. London, 1968.

Ornstein, Robert. "Marlowe and God: The Tragic Theology of *Doctor Faustus*." *PMLA* 83 (1968): 1378–85.

Palmer, D. J. "Marlowe's Naturalism." In *Christopher Marlowe.* Ed. Brian Morris. London, 1968.

Poirer, Michel. *Christopher Marlowe.* London, 1951.

Ribner, Irving. *The English History Play in the Age of Shakespeare.* London, 1965.

———. "The Idea of History in Marlowe's *Tamburlaine*." *Journal of English Literary History* 20 (1953): 251–66.

———. "Marlowe's 'Tragicke Glasse.'" In *Essays on Shakespeare and Elizabethan Drama.* Ed. Richard Hosley. Columbia, Mo., 1962.

———. "Significance of Gentillet's Contre-Machiavel." *Modern Language Quarterly* 10 (1949): 153–57.

Seaton, Ethel. "Fresh Sources for Marlowe." *Review of English Studies* 5 (1929): 385–401.

———. "Marlowe's Map." *Essays and Studies* 10 (1924): 13–35.

Spivack, Bernard. *Shakespeare and the Allegory of Evil.* New York, 1958.

Steane, J. B. *Marlowe: A Critical Study*. Cambridge, England, 1965.

Waith, Eugene. *"Edward II*: The Shadow of Action." *Tulane Drama Review* 4 (1964):59–76.

Wickham, Glynne. *Shakespeare's Dramatic Heritage*. London, 1969.

Wilson, F. P. *Marlowe and the Early Shakespeare*. Oxford, 1953.

————. *Shakespearean and Other Studies*. Ed. Helen Gardner. Oxford, 1969.

INDEX

3